TRADE PROPERLY

Copyright © 2024 Thomas Kohler
All rights reserved.
ISBN-13: 979-8-8796-1826-6

TRADE PROPERLY

THOMAS KOHLER

I dedicate this book to my dear parents,

as well as to you, dear reader, in recognition of your commitment to improving your life.

INTRODUCTION TO TRADING 19

How much capital to start trading? 20

Overview of instruments 21

Stocks 24
Dividends
Emission of shares
Splits

Exchange-traded funds 31
Passive investing
Diversification
Performances
Compound interests

Leveraged ETFs 43
Beta slippage
The risk of leveraged ETFs
Performances

REIT 50

Bonds 53
Safe haven
Maturity curve
ETF of bonds

Forex 59

Cryptocurrencies 59

Commodities 62

Alternative investments 63

Inflation 64

Styles of trading	66
How to trade?	68
Analyze charts	
Broker	
Types of orders	69
Market order	
Limit order	
Stop order	
Take-profit and stop-loss	
GTC and GFD	
Short selling	
Who owns stocks?	76
Risk and uncertainty	77
Decision-making with risk	
Decision-making with uncertainty	
Vocabulary	83

FUNDAMENTAL ANALYSIS — 87

The price	87
Value & Growth	89
Value investing	
Growth investing	
Value vs. Growth investing	
The book value	92
Price-to-book ratio	
Book value per share	
P/E ratio	100
Piotroski score	102

The fundamental analysis that no one talks about	105

MANAGING TRADES — 107

Diversification — 108
Asset classes

Risk reward ratio — 115
Getting rid of potential losses

Lump-sum investing vs Dollar-cost averaging — 119
Mixed approach
Price & time approach

Do the opposite — 125

The emotion of the market — 127
The VIX
The Fear and Greed Index
The DXY
The medias

Missing the train — 130

There is no one best way — 131

Margins — 131

Protecting your account — 133

PERSONAL FINANCE — 135

Compensating vs growing — 135

Assessing your current financial situation — 137
Performance overview

Expenses — 143

TECHNICAL ANALYSIS — 149

Trends and ranges — 150
Dow's theory

Candlesticks — 152
Interpretations

Candlestick patterns — 158

Heikin Ashi — 161

Supports and resistances — 163

Breakouts — 166
False breakouts
Pullbacks and throwbacks

Gaps — 170
Common gap
Breakaway gap
Runaway gap or Measuring gap
Exhaustion gap
Island reversal

Manipulation — 180

Momentum indicators — 182
Period
The Relative strength index
Choppiness index
RSI vs CHOP

Moving averages — 191
Periods for moving avengers
Other types of moving averages

Ichimoku cloud — 203

Fibonacci 206
Fibonacci retracement
Fibonacci time zones
Fibonacci as periods
My secret for periods
Multiplying

Elliott Wave Theory 221

Anchored VWAP 223

Chart patterns 224
The effect of timeframes on patterns
Double top / bottom
Triple top / bottom
Head and shoulders
Wedge
Boardening wedge
Right-angled boardening wedge
Diamond
Triangle
Continuation chart patterns

Final advices 252

When it comes to wealth creation, the path to financial freedom can often appear convoluted. Most people have a misguided perception of their potential to earn money. We can all become wealthy, not necessarily by working hard, but rather by doing the right things. My journey and ambition for wealth began at the age of 12 when I believed the only path to become a multimillionaire was becoming a CEO. I thought I needed an extraordinary idea to create an extraordinary business. However, I later realized that investors are the real winners, not the CEO's. While running a company certainly requires hard work, investors are free from daily operational work and responsibilities.

Indeed, note that financial freedom does not encompass freedom in its entirety. Opting for the path of an investor entails sacrificing some security, but the potential gain in overall life freedom could be unimaginably greater. Investors wield the power to dictate when, where and how much they engage in their "work".

Instead of building an extraordinary business, you have the option to simply invest in extraordinary businesses.

"Will your own business be greater than the best ones you can find?" If your answer is yes, then a follow-up question arises: "Are the additional profitability and security you gain from running your own business worth the effort?" If you answer yes again, then you may not need to read this book. But if you decide to become an investor, however, this book is meant for you.

Welcome to the gateway of investment, a realm that remains frustratingly elusive for many, largely due to false beliefs. This book is designed to serve as the key to that gateway, empowering you not only to achieve financial freedom but also to gain freedom in life, as investing is the path to both.

While money certainly isn't everything, it undeniably wields the power to acquire a wide array of desires, from yachts and Lamborghinis to fame and respect. In our current world, there are two universal languages: English and money. So, don't feel guilty for desiring financial success; it is simply the way our world operates.

By reading this book, I promise that you will become part of the elite 1% who possess profound knowledge of trading and investing.

Now, let's bring ourselves back to reality: the truth is that the majority of traders end up losing money.

The initial mistake that many individuals make is to try to trade rather than invest. In essence, they believe that the more they trade, the more money they will make. Consequently, their actions resemble pure gambling rather than adhering to a logical long-term investment approach.

The second mistake they frequently commit is placing their hopes in the outcome. It's a common human tendency to be swayed by emotions, but succumbing to impulses can be detrimental in the investing world. Indeed, when emotions take the reins, you are highly likely to do the exact opposite of what you should be doing. I couldn't help but chuckle when I witnessed half of my fellow university peers investing in cryptocurrencies back in 2022. It wasn't necessarily because it was an inherently poor decision, but rather due to the intensity of their greed. Trading cannot be approached in such manners, it is far from a game. Your decisions must be guided by the utmost wisdom. How could it not be that way?

Let me ask you something: Do you take your life seriously or not? Because we won't play with money here. Our mission is to achieve long-term wealth by following a proper and safe path. To become a successful trader, you must embody crucial qualities: patience, discipline and self-honesty. It is equally important to be prepared for the possibility of losses.

This book is designed to cater to both beginner and intermediate traders. In the initial sections, we will cover all the basic aspects, gradually delving deeper into investments. The last chapter will teach advanced trading techniques based on charts that may help you enhance your investments. Therefore, if the beginning seems overly simplistic to you, there's no need to worry. The book's purpose is to ensure that every reader reaches a high level of trading – the proper trading. Let's begin.

"An investment in knowledge pays the best interest."

- Benjamin Franklin, Founding father of the United States.

First part

INTRODUCTION TO TRADING

Welcome to the opening chapter. In this section, we will summarize the fundamental aspects that define trading and investing. We will explore the most common financial instruments you can use and provide you with essential knowledge to kickstart your trading journey. Beginners will find these sections valuable as they provide foundational knowledge. However, if you already have a solid understanding of the assets and upcoming information, feel free to skip ahead to more advanced sections.

To commence, let's distinguish between two crucial concepts: investing and trading.

Investing involves allocating resources—often money—with the expectation of seeing profitable returns or an increase in value over time. Investors engage in a variety of asset classes, including stocks, bonds, real estate and mutual funds, aiming for long-term financial growth or wealth preservation.

Trading, on the other hand, involves actively buying and selling financial instruments to profit from short-term price movements. In contrast to the longer-term perspective of investing, trading seeks gains from market fluctuations occurring over shorter timeframes, ranging from seconds to months. Essentially, trading is the art of capitalizing on price differences through strategic buying and selling.

How much capital to start trading?

If you're good at investing or trading, achieving a yearly income of x typically necessitates an initial investment of at least 5x. Despite claims from some influencers suggesting otherwise, commencing trading with a mere $100 or even $500 may not be realistic. For a trading endeavor to be meaningful and worthwhile, a capital of at least $5000 will be required at some point.

Now, don't worry if you currently have less than $5000. Starting your trading journey with a low sum is still a viable option and far better than not starting at all. In this scenario, the key is to diligently save whatever amount you can each month. Consider contributing, for instance, $200 monthly to your trading account. As we'll explore later, leveraging the power of compound interest will become your greatest ally on this journey.

Overview of instruments

Now, let's explore some common financial instruments you'll encounter in the trading world. These instruments will be explored more thoroughly in the following chapters.

- **Stocks:** Ownership in a company.

- **Bonds:** Loans extended to governments or companies, typically with fixed payments.

- **Exchange-Traded Funds (ETFs):** Baskets of different securities, such as collections of stocks.

- **Currencies (Forex):** Exchanging different currencies.

- **Cryptocurrencies:** Digital assets using cryptography for security and transaction verification.

- **Commodities:** Essential goods or raw materials like oil, gold, natural gas and agricultural products.

- **Options:** Contracts granting the buyer the right (but not the obligation) to buy or sell an underlying asset at a certain price within a specified timeframe.

- **Futures:** Contracts to buy or sell an underlying asset at a predetermined price on a specific future date.

Note that options and futures are more suitable for experienced traders due to their complexity.

For beginners, it is advisable to concentrate on **stocks**, **bonds** and their corresponding **ETFs**. Stocks represent ownership in companies and well-managed companies tend to generate profits and increase in value over time. Regarding bonds, they offer a predictable and almost guaranteed income through interest payments.

The key point emphasized here is that certain assets have an inherent wealth-generating nature, while others do not. Stocks and bonds, in particular, have a track record of delivering long-term returns, in contrast to most commodities and currencies whose values are not naturally inclined to increase.

When you invest in Bitcoin or gold for instance, your expectation is reliant on the hope that the next person will be willing to pay more than you did. In contrast, owning stocks of a company means investing in the production of tangible output or services from that particular business. This fundamental distinction underscores the difference between speculative investments and those that involve a direct stake in the production of something.

For now, just remember that the following assets are the ones you should focus on because they are truly meant to generate income:

- Stocks

- Bonds

- ETFs of stocks

- ETFs of bonds

The upcoming sections will delve into a more comprehensive exploration of the key assets you need to be familiar with.

At the core of understanding the use of stocks and bonds is the recognition that many companies have aspirations to invest beyond the limitations of their own resources. In order to obtain immediate capital for expansion, they have three primary options available:

- Borrow money (taking loans from banks)

- Issue bonds

- Issue stocks

Stocks

A stock, often referred to as a share when talking about a specific company, represents ownership in a company. Buying a stock makes you a shareholder, which essentially means you own a piece of that company.

Motivations for businesses

Companies issue stocks as a way to raise capital for various purposes, such as expanding their operations, launching new products, or reducing debt.

Motivations for the shareholder

By purchasing stocks, you are essentially saying, "Here's my money; invest it in your company so you can grow". In return, you receive a share of the company, which may lead to potential capital gains if the stock's value increases over time. Additionally, companies may distribute a portion of their profits to shareholders through what's called dividends.

Imagine buying 10% of a land and the next day people find out that this land has much gold in it. So if the value of the land doubled, then your 10% also did.

The same principle applies to stocks: you own a fixed portion of a company, but the value of that portion can fluctuate.

There are four main reasons to invest in stocks:

- To support the company.

- To gain voting rights in the company.

- To benefit from potential increases in the company's value, which can lead to a higher stock price.

- To receive dividends.

Dividends

As mentioned earlier, a company may choose to distribute a portion of its profits to shareholders in the form of dividends. This is a way to thank them for supporting the company and can also attract more investors.

Dividends can be paid out in various ways, such as a percentage of the share price in cash or in the form of additional shares. A company can choose to issue dividends periodically or not and decides on the amount it wants to distribute.

Some traders compare dividends when selecting companies to invest in, favoring those that offer consistent and high dividend payouts.

However, with regard to dividends, many investors ignore the following principles. It's important to understand that when dividends are paid out, the share's value of the company often reduces proportionally. This is because once a company distributes a dividend, there is no more dividend to expect for some time, which reduces the value of the share. Additionally, a dividend is a transfer of value from the company you bet on to the shareholders. Therefore, the fact that the company sends money to every shareholder is a zero-sum equation as it loses its money (your money) to give it back to you.

In the case of companies issuing additional shares as dividends rather than money, a similar principle applies. Indeed, increasing the number of existing shares can cause the stock price to drop proportionally following the law of supply and demand. In simpler terms, as the company gives more shares to every shareholder, the value per share will decrease.

In short, what dividends make you earn will be negatively compensated in the price of the share. From this theoretical point of view, despite what most people think, dividends do not increase investors' overall profit. It is even possible to consider that they reduce it, as the money goes to investors and is not reinvested for the company's growth.

However, while dividends may somehow be compensated in the stock price, they can provide a steady stream of income for investors over the long-term. This is what truly makes them somehow valuable for those seeking to earn more regular returns on their investments, even in times of market volatility.

In conclusion, dividends give a misleading impression of returns. You do indeed receive money or more shares, but this reduces the share's price almost proportionally. It also reduces the company's inner investment. Therefore, the fact that a company issues dividends can roughly be considered as neutral regarding profit.

Emission of shares

The terms "emit" or "issue" have been mentioned in previous sections. Let's explore how this process works.

Companies can issue shares into the market through two means:

- An Initial Public Offering (IPO)

- A secondary offering

An IPO is the first time a company emits its shares into the primary market, meaning that they are directly purchased from the company. It marks the first public commercialization of its shares. Once the IPO is completed, meaning the initial buyers have acquired their shares, those shares are traded in what is known as the secondary market.

Given the number of shares the company decided to emit, professional analysts determine the price of the IPO based on calculations that vary for each company. However, the IPO price may not reflect the actual supply and demand in the secondary market, which can be influenced by various factors. This can result in a risky investment for beginners, as share prices may fluctuate greatly in the initial period following the offering.

Once the IPO is done, companies can also emit new shares into the market through a secondary offering. This is when they offer additional shares to the public after the IPO. Note that it is also possible for the company to buy its own shares.

You might understand that when I said "you own a fixed portion of a company", it wasn't totally right, as the number of emitted shares (called number of shares outstanding) can vary slightly. These variations are caused by secondary offerings, the company buying its shares back, or also because of dividends that are paid with shares.

Splits

Over time, as a company grows and becomes more valuable, the value of its shares will also increase. But at some point, the price of one share can become too high, for example, $2000.

In this case, to make their stock more affordable to a wider range of investors, companies sometimes decide to do what is called a stock split. A stock split occurs when a company increases the number of outstanding shares by dividing each share into multiple shares. For instance, if a company has 1 million outstanding shares and decides to implement a 2-for-1 stock split, shareholders would then possess 2 million shares, but the value of each share would be divided by 2. By splitting the shares and reducing the price per share, more investors may be enticed to buy in, leading to increased demand for the stock and potentially driving up the price.

Another reason for a stock split is to enhance liquidity. When a company has a small number of outstanding shares, it can be difficult to find buyers and sellers for each individual share. By splitting its shares and increasing the number of outstanding shares, a company enhances liquidity and the flow of exchanges.

Overall, a stock split is simply a way for a company to make its stock more accessible. However, it's important to note that a stock split does not change the underlying value of the company; it simply adjusts the number of outstanding shares and the price per share.

It is, therefore, important to distinguish the emission of shares covered in the previous section and splits. The sole reason stock splits can have an impact is the increased accessibility of the shares.

Lastly, it's also worth noting that splits can be either forward or reverse. A forward split increases the number of shares outstanding and reduces the price, while a reverse split decreases the number of shares outstanding to increase the price per share.

Exchange-traded funds

ETFs, or exchange-traded funds, are a type of investment fund that holds a basket of underlying assets, such as stocks, bonds, or commodities. Despite their potential to be up to 2 times more profitable than real estate, ETFs remain unknown to many people.

Unlike traditional mutual funds, ETFs are traded on an exchange, like individual stocks and their prices can fluctuate throughout the day. This flexibility makes them more accessible for investors who want to buy or sell shares at any time during market hours.

In simple terms, investing in ETFs allows investors to buy shares in a diversified portfolio of assets with a single transaction. For instance, if you want to invest in the 100 biggest tech companies in the United States, you can simply buy one ETF that tracks them.

Indexes commonly serve as benchmarks for ETFs, making ETFs a way for investors to invest in an index. An index is a calculation that provides information about a group of financial assets that share common characteristics, such as value, industry, country, or size.

Various types of indexes are available, each tracking a specific group of financial assets. One of the most widely followed indexes is the S&P 500 (Standard & Poor's 500), consisting of the 500 largest companies in the United States. The S&P 500 index is considered a benchmark for the overall US stock market's performance and many ETFs are designed to track its performance.

Below are the top 10 companies held in this ETF as of the time of writing:

ID of the company in the stock market — Symbol
Percentage of that company in the ETF — Weight
Current price of one share — Price

#	Company	Symbol	Weight	Price
1	Apple Inc.	AAPL	6.802701	▲ 173.28
2	Microsoft Corporation	MSFT	5.800789	▲ 310.20
3	Amazon.com Inc.	AMZN	3.564757	▼ 3,239.00
4	Tesla Inc	TSLA	2.127035	▼ 1,045.10
5	Alphabet Inc. Class A	GOOGL	2.113449	▼ 2,785.00
6	Alphabet Inc. Class C	GOOG	1.972093	▼ 2,795.11
7	Meta Platforms Inc. Class A	FB	1.958212	▲ 332.14
8	NVIDIA Corporation	NVDA	1.684118	▼ 268.85
9	Berkshire Hathaway Inc. Class B	BRK.B	1.491286	▲ 324.13
10	JPMorgan Chase & Co.	JPM	1.260167	▲ 157.89

Within the ETF, Apple holds a weight of 6.8%. Therefore, if an investor buys $100 worth of an S&P500 ETF and the value of Apple's shares drops by 50%, the investor would experience a loss of $3.4.

Passive investing

Passive investing is a long-term investment strategy in which investors retain their assets for an extended period without frequent buying or selling. ETFs serve as an ideal option for passive investing, designed to track a specific index and automatically adjust holdings as the index changes.

This eliminates the necessity for investors to take additional actions, as all required trades to stay current with the index are executed for them. By investing in an ETF, investors can be confident that they are investing in the best stocks according to the index's criteria, without the need for constant monitoring and trades.

In other words, poorly performing companies leave the portfolio and strong-performing ones join and automatically remain in it. This approach eliminates the need to pick individual stocks, a task that can be challenging to predict over the long term.

"If you pick an individual stock, who knows if it will still be doing well in 20 years? But if you buy an ETF, you will, at all times, be investing in the best stocks according to the index's criteria."

Diversification

The second best characteristic of ETFs is the diversification they offer. Diversification is the practice of investing in a range of assets to reduce global the risk of a portfolio. ETFs provide diversification by tracking an index, which is composed of multiple stocks or assets. By investing in an ETF, you are essentially buying a basket of stocks, bonds, or other assets, reducing the impact of any poor performing asset on the overall portfolio. This makes ETFs inherently less volatile than individual stocks, providing investors with a more stable and diversified investment option.

In the example mentioned earlier, we lost only $3.4 with a diversified portfolio, but we would have lost $50 if we had only owned Apple's stock. This highlights the importance of diversification in protecting your wealth. ETFs, by nature, offer less volatility than individual stocks, making them an excellent option for investors looking for stable long-term investments.

By diversifying your investments through an ETF, you can spread your risk and increase your chances of achieving steady returns over time. It's a simple yet powerful way to protect your wealth.

Performances

Historically, the US stock market has been the most profitable. While there is no guarantee that it will continue to perform at such a high level, the long-term trend is generally positive. Investing in an ETF that tracks a well-diversified index of US stocks can provide a solid return on investment over time.

If you are skeptical about the future performance of the US stock market, you may consider investing in a global ETF that tracks stocks from a variety of countries, or in an ETF that tracks the stock market of a country or region that you have confidence in.

In addition, ETFs generally have lower fees compared to other investment options such as mutual funds or actively managed funds. This is because ETFs are typically passively managed, meaning they aim to track an index rather than relying on an active fund manager to make decisions on which stocks to buy and sell. The lower fees make ETFs an attractive option for investors seeking cost-effective exposure to a diversified portfolio. If investors were to purchase, on their own, the individual shares represented in an ETF, they might incur much higher commission fees than those associated with buying and selling ETFs.

In summary, ETFs provide investors with an excellent opportunity to diversify their portfolio, benefit from strong performances and minimize fees, all this with a very passive approach.

Here are four of the most well-known and popular ETFs in the United States. I do not like the last one but I shall explain why in the next chapter.

SPDR S&P 500 ETF

Symbol	Benchmark	Annual return
SPY	S&P 500 Index	+10,14% (1995-2020)

Components

500 large-cap US stocks covering about 80% of the total US equities market capitalization

Invesco QQQ Trust

Symbol	Benchmark	Annual return
QQQ	Nasdaq-100 Index	+13.11% (1995-2020)

Components

100 largest non-financial companies listed on the Nasdaq Stock Market

iShares Russell 2000 ETF

Symbol	Benchmark	Annual return
IWM	Russell 2000 Index	+7.93% (2000-2020)

Components

2000 small-cap US stocks, market cap between $300 million and $2 billion

Dow Jones Industrial Average ETF

Symbol	Benchmark	Annual return
DIA	D.J.I.A.	+7.00% (2000-2022)

Components

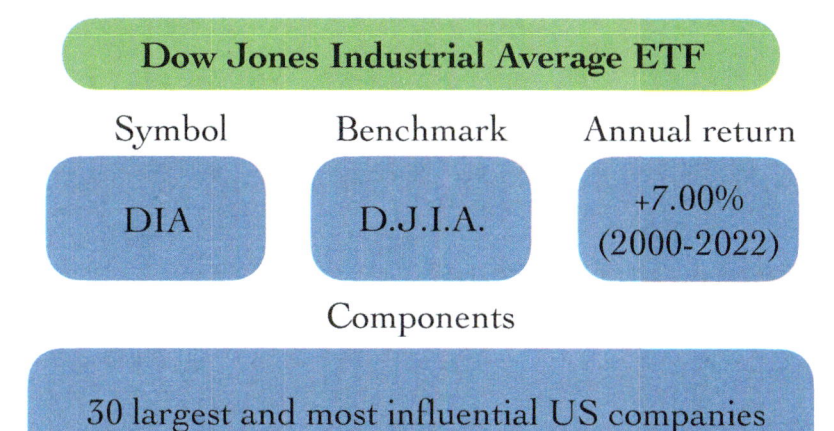

30 largest and most influential US companies

It's important to emphasize the distinction between indexes and ETFs. While indexes themselves are not directly purchasable, you can invest in them by purchasing an ETF that tracks a specific index. In addition to the examples I've provided, there are numerous other ETF providers available. Keep in mind that while fees for ETFs are generally low, they may vary slightly from one provider to another. Diversifying your ETF providers could be interesting to reduce your risk, but it's crucial to select providers with a strong reputation.

Based on assets under management, the two largest ETF providers globally are BlackRock's iShares and Vanguard. By visiting their websites, you can explore a wide variety of ETFs that track everything from small-cap to emerging markets, specific countries and even thematic ETFs like those related to the Metaverse for instance. Other providers that you may find interesting include Amundi and Lyxor.

Compound interests

"Compound interest is the eighth wonder of the world. He who understands it, earns it; he who doesn't, pays it."

- Albert Einstein

Compound interest is a powerful tool in investing that can help you build wealth over time. It involves earning interest not only on your initial investment but also on any accumulated interest from previous periods. As a result, your investment can grow exponentially over time.

In trading, compound interest can work in your favor if you reinvest your profits. For example, if you make a 30% profit on a $10,000 investment, you will have $13,000. If you reinvest all and make another 30% profit, you will have $16,900 instead of $16,000 if you do not reinvest. As insignificant as it may seem, this compounding effect can lead to significant returns over time. The graph below can provide a better understanding.

+30% per year starting at $10.000

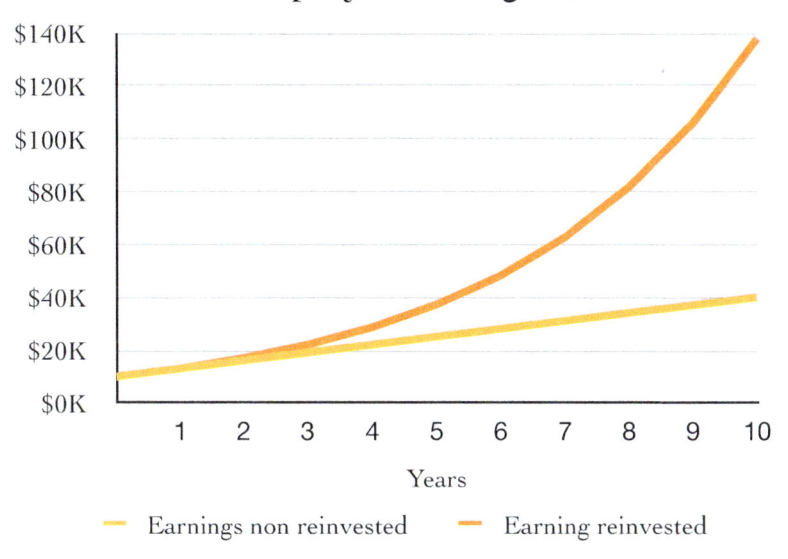

The main lesson conveyed by this graph is as follows: The initial efforts always appear impressively insignificant. In this case, you can observe that during the first three years, life seemed the same for both reinvesting and non-reinvesting investors.

In the example presented, the non-reinvested capital initially enjoyed by investors in the first three years amounted to $2,970. However, after 10 years, the investor who reinvested their profits was able to make the same amount in just 26 days. This highlights the power of compounding and the importance of reinvesting profits in trading.

If you wish to have a concrete example, consider investing $100,000 in the Nasdaq 100 Index (QQQ) in 1985. By 2020, your investment would have grown to over $8.8 million, without any additional effort on your part – no rent, no work, just one click and wait.

Going further, if you consider daily goals, you will probably be stunned of the low performances you need to make. There are 252 days of trading per year, if you get to do +0,25% every day, you'll reach a performance of +87,6% per year. At this rate, you can go from $10.000 to **$2.9 billions** in 20 years.

In conclusion, beginners should consider starting with ETFs, which offer low risk and consistently strong performance. Starting early is especially important, as even small investments can compound into significant wealth over time.

Keep in mind this crucial rule:

"It always seems insignificant in the first years."

The effects of certain actions or decisions may not be immediately apparent, but they can accumulate over time and have a significant impact on your overall success. However, it is impossible to have good performances every year; keep in mind that the market has a huge volatility.

"The best moment for you to invest was when you were born; the second best moment is now, as insignificant as it may look."

Leveraged ETFs

Leveraged ETFs can be an appealing option for investors seeking amplified returns on their investments. These ETFs utilize financial leverage to multiply the returns of the underlying assets in the fund. Put simply, leveraged ETFs aim to deliver returns that are two, three, or even five times greater than the returns of a standard ETF.

There are two types of leveraged ETFs: long and short. If you own a long leveraged ETF, such as a X5 leveraged ETF, your daily performance will be five times larger than that of the base ETF. For example, if the base ETF earns 1% within a day, you would earn 5% instead. Conversely, if you own a short X5 leveraged ETF, you would have made a -5% return while the base ETF performed positively at 1%.

I strongly advise against buying short leveraged ETFs, as they go against the natural long-term uptrend of the market.

All of this may sound very appealing, but don't rush into it yet because everything in finance is a double-edged sword.

Beta slippage

Understanding the unique characteristics of leveraged ETFs is crucial, particularly the concept of beta slippage. Beta slippage refers to a multi-day tracking inefficiency that affects leveraged funds. This discrepancy occurs because leveraged ETFs are designed to replicate daily returns and to achieve this, they require periodic rebalancing to maintain their desired level of leverage. Due to the daily compounding effect, the long-term returns of leveraged ETFs are misaligned with the performance of their underlying benchmark.

Legend

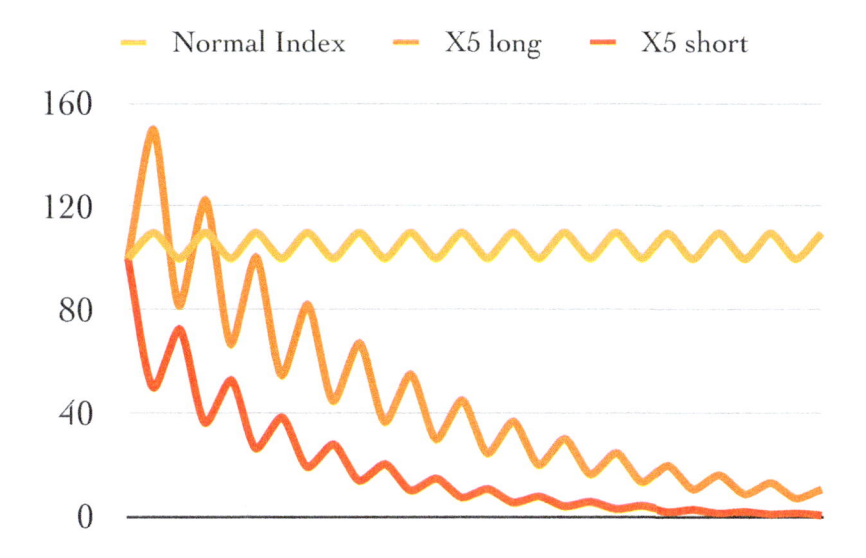

— Normal Index   — X5 long   — X5 short

Leveraged ETFs are theoretically not intended for long-term investments. Instead, they are designed to be held for a single day.

The deviation resulting from the daily compounding effect of the leveraged ETF depends on the volatility and trend of the underlying asset. If the benchmark experiences frequent fluctuations in price, the leveraged ETF will tend towards 0. However, if the benchmark exhibits a steady upward trend over an extended period, a leveraged ETF will outperform its benchmark's performance multiplied by the leverage factor over time.

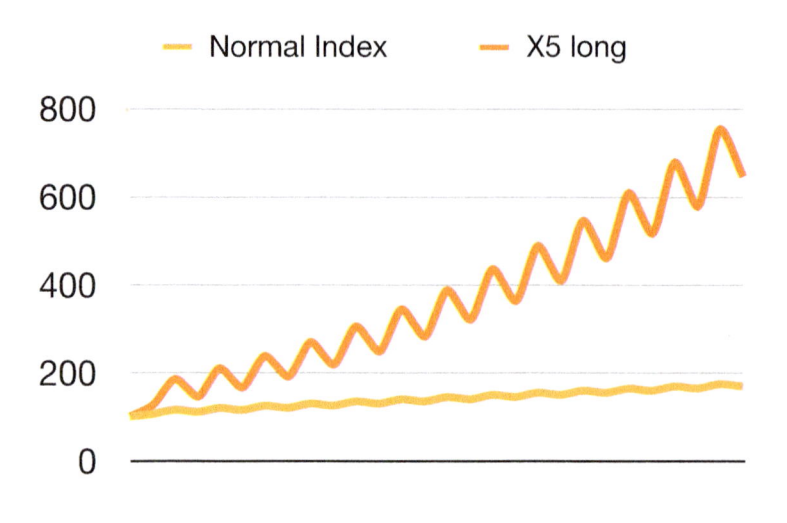

— Normal Index   — X5 long

800
600
400
200
0

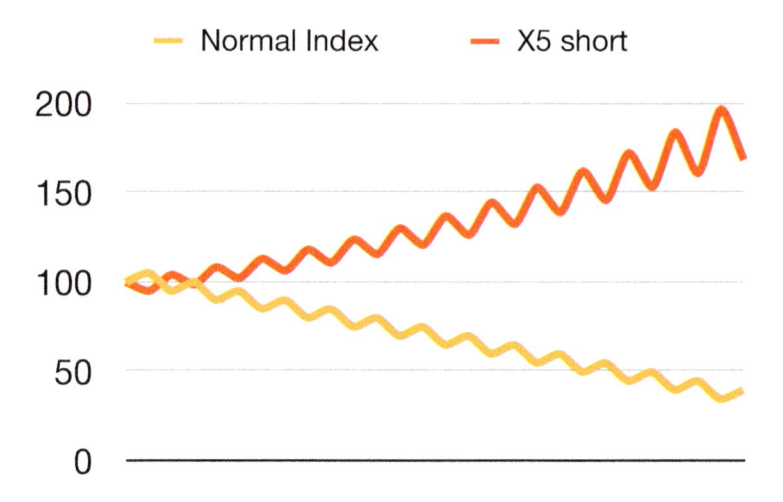

— Normal Index   — X5 short

200
150
100
50
0

The risk of leveraged ETFs

You might be wondering what happens to your ✕3 ETF if the underlying drops by more than 33.3%.

Technically, the only scenario in which an ETF may go below zero is when the significant drop occurs in a single day, for example, -34% in a single day for the ✕3 leveraged ETF. However, such an event is unlikely.

Even if we consider a scenario where the benchmark loses 10% every day for 10 days, it would still be above zero, despite the leverage.

Note that, by the time I write this book, the three biggest daily drops of the DJIA (Dow Jones Industrial Average) ever recorded since 1900 were respectively -22.61%, -12.93% and -12.82%. Therefore, as a precaution, it's advisable to avoid leverages higher than ✕3 in our investments.

Performances

By saying "theoretically" when I mentioned that these ETFs are not meant to be used in long-term investing it's because some have a mind-blowing long term performance. We're talking about 30% to 50% per year on average with a ✕3 leverage.

For instance, UPRO, an S&P500 ✗3 long ETF provided by ProShares, witnessed a remarkable growth from $2.91 in January 2011 to $38.87 in January 2021. This represents a multiplication of its price by more than 13 in 10 years, translating to an almost +30% per year.

As to TQQQ, a NASDAQ-100 ✗3 long ETF, it went from $0.79 to $46.02 within the same period. That's a ✗58 performance, representing more than 50% per year.

This is not a recommendation to buy these ETFs. I'm simply sharing facts and powerful trading elements. You must know that very few leveraged ETFs show great long term performances. It is, in fact, pretty unthinkable to introduce leveraged ETFs in such an introductory chapter, as these are complex products and can generate great losses. You must therefore keep in mind that these ETFs have crazy volatility, making them difficult to handle for the average Joe. If you do decide to invest in these ETFs, it's crucial to select them wisely, considering diversified components and only big and famous indexes. The main goal would be to avoid ETFs that are not diversified enough, meaning that they could have a significant drop in a very short period.

Note that few of them have a good long term performance, decreasing gradually as we have seen in the previous graph.

An investment exclusively based on leveraged ETFs is not suitable for any investor. It is necessary to always have normal ETFs within your portfolio and, if possible, poorly related to the country of your leveraged ETFs.

In conclusion, taking into consideration the previous section on compound interest, leveraged ETFs have the potential to generate remarkable returns and offer an interesting way to use margins. On the other hand, it is important to remember that leveraged ETFs tend to deviate significantly from the returns of their benchmark. Additionally, their high volatility poses a considerable challenge for the majority of individuals and these complex assets are intended solely for highly experienced and capable investors. I do not recommend them to everyone; individuals should thoroughly understand the risks involved. Lastly, let me remind you that you should never exceed a leverage of 3.

REIT

This section should in fact be part of the "Stocks" chapter, but there were some elements to settle down before.

Real estate holds a certain appeal for many individuals, although I must admit that I am not its biggest enthusiast. This is primarily due to my conviction that the stock market tends to yield superior results with less effort. Their only con is the volatility. It is, however, always interesting to diversify your wealth and as real estate satisfies a lot of people, you must, therefore, know that it is possible to invest in real estate through the stock market.

Real Estate Investment Trusts (REITs) are companies that own, operate, or finance real estate properties. There are also ETFs available that focus on investing in REITs.

While volatility is still a factor in the stock market, purchasing stocks is considerably easier compared to the complex procedures involved in real estate transactions. With online trading, there is no need for physical paperwork or client interactions. It is also accessible to individuals with lower capital and you can rely on professional companies to manage the investments on your behalf. What more could you ask for?

If this interests you, you can start by checking out these ETFs.

iShares Global REIT ETF

Symbol	Benchmark	Annual return
REET	FTSE EPRA/NAREIT Global REIT	+3.00% (1995-2020)

Components

REITs in both developed and emerging markets worldwide

iShares Core U.S. REIT ETF

Symbol: USRT

Benchmark: FTSE Nareit Equity REITs

Annual return: +8.58% (1995-2020)

Components: U.S. publicly traded equity REITs

Bonds

Bonds are debt securities issued by companies or governments as a way to borrow money. When you buy a bond, you are lending money to the issuer in exchange for fixed interest payments over a specified period of time. At the end of this period, the bond's face value is repaid.

In simpler words, a bond consists in three steps.

- You pay the capital (N) (called nominal).

- You receive a periodic interest (i) during the whole life of the bond (called coupon).

- You receive your nominal (N) back when it ends.

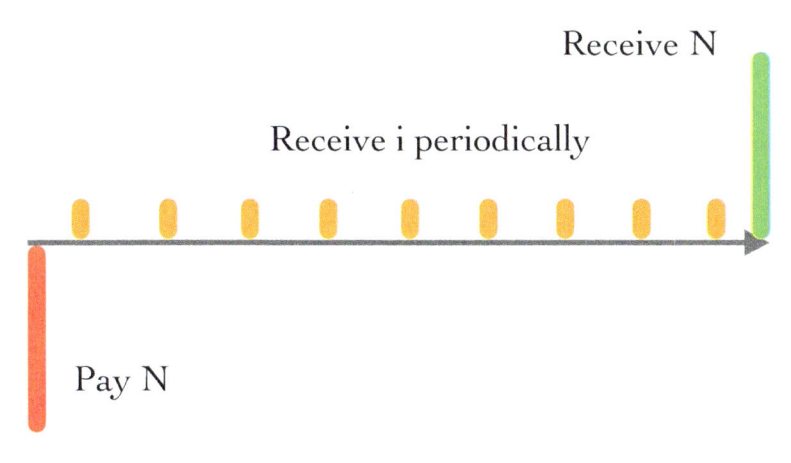

Receive N

Receive i periodically

Pay N

It's important to note that bonds can be sold before their maturity date. The price at which they can be sold depends on various factors such as changes in interest rates, inflation and credit risk. For example, if interest rates rise after you purchase a bond, its value may decrease because new bonds with higher interest rates will be more attractive to investors.

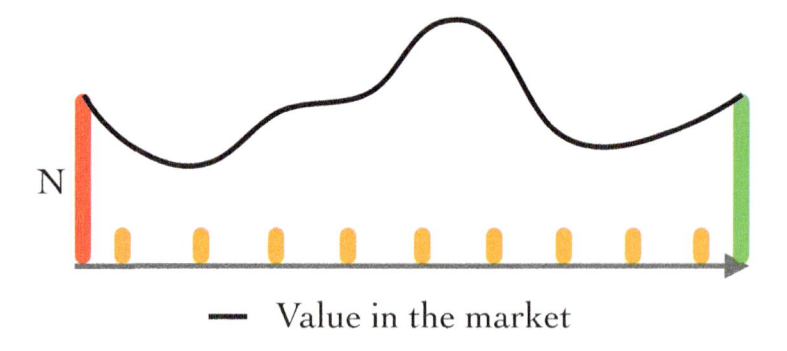

— Value in the market

After your purchase, as new bonds with different interest rates emerge, the value of your bond will move accordingly. However, when the bond reaches the end of its life, its value in the market returns to the nominal amount. The reason for this is that there are no more (or few) interest payments remaining and you will receive the nominal amount. In summary, a bond starts its life and ends its life at the nominal value, usually 100.

Safe haven

In times of economic uncertainty or market volatility, bonds are often considered a safe haven asset. Investors, seeking perceived safety, are willing to pay a premium, leading to an increase in bond prices. Bonds, esteemed for preserving wealth and yielding consistent profits, offer a relatively secure haven in the realm of investments. Despite their lower potential returns compared to riskier assets, bonds provide a dependable source of fixed income.

Maturity curve

The key risk associated with bonds is credit risk, hinging on the possibility of not recovering the invested funds if the issuing entity, whether a company or government, encounters financial distress or bankruptcy. Risk and reward share a crucial relationship in bonds. The greater the risk a bond carries, the more enticing the interest it must promise. This correlation is why bonds with longer maturities frequently yield higher interest rates. The logic is simple: the more extended the journey to maturity, the greater the credit risks. Consequently, bonds with extended maturities sweeten the deal for investors with elevated interest rates. This dynamic is encapsulated by the maturity curve, offering investors a tool to compare interest rates across different maturities.

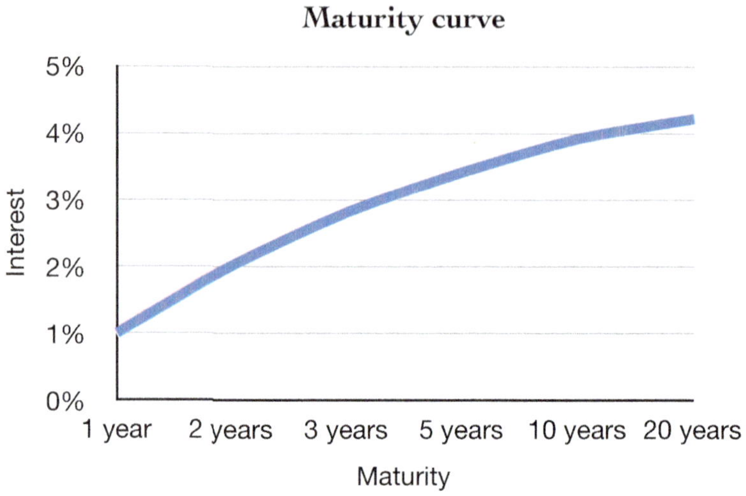
Maturity curve
5%
4%
3%
2%
1%
0%
Interest
1 year
2 years
3 years
5 years
10 years
20 years
Maturity

The curve's shape provides insights into the current market perception, reflecting investors' expectations. It is predominantly influenced by both perceived credit risk and anticipated rates for future bonds.

Steep or Normal Curve

When short-term rates are lower than long-term rates, we have a steep or normal yield curve. Long-term bonds offer higher interest rates than short-term bonds. The risks associated with holding bonds over a long period, such as inflation risk, demand a higher income or yield. Investors indicate their expectation of continuous economic growth without major interruptions. Therefore, they are more inclined to engage in long-term investments.

Flat Yield Curve

When short-term rates are only slightly lower than long-term rates, a flat yield curve emerges. This indicates that investors expect a reduction in inflation and more moderate future economic growth. Short-term and long-term yields are at similar levels, suggests that the economy is in a transition period.

Inverted Yield Curve

Finally, when short-term rates are higher than long-term rates, an inverted yield curve forms. Investors generally do not appreciate inverted yield curves. This curve seems counterintuitive but is explainable. Investors, concerned about short-term prospects, demand a higher income for holding investments with shorter maturities. Lower interest rates typically signify weaker economic growth and an inverted yield curve may indicate an impending recession. Such a shape suggests that a sharp economic slowdown is anticipated, constituting a scenario in which inflation would decrease.

ETF of bonds

ETFs of bonds offer investors exposure to a diversified portfolio of bonds. These ETFs may invest in various types of bonds, including government, corporate and municipal bonds. Coupons are usually directly integrated into the price of the underlying bond. One well-known bond ETF is the iShares 20+ Year Treasury Bond ETF (TLT), which tracks the performance of U.S. Treasury bonds with maturities of 20 years or more.

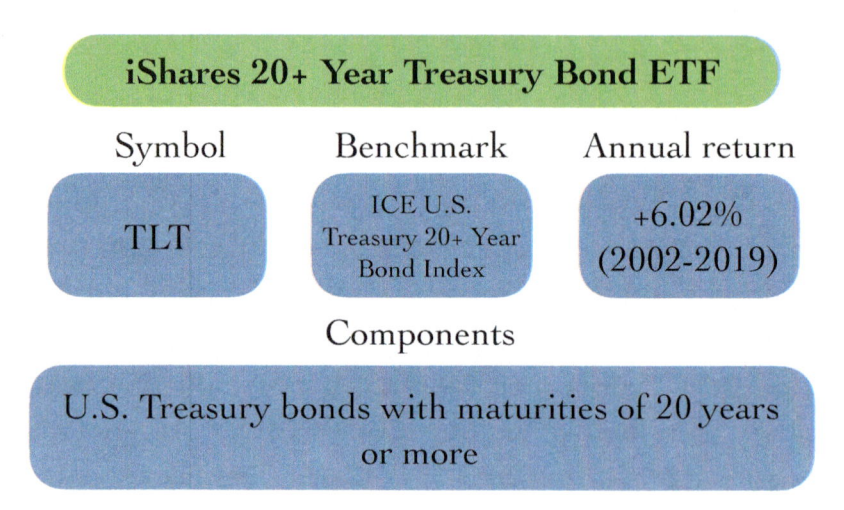

iShares 20+ Year Treasury Bond ETF

Symbol	Benchmark	Annual return
TLT	ICE U.S. Treasury 20+ Year Bond Index	+6.02% (2002-2019)

Components

U.S. Treasury bonds with maturities of 20 years or more

In summary, bond ETFs offer a simple and efficient way to invest in bonds. They are also perpetual, as new bonds are purchased whenever the current ones reach their maturity.

Forex

Forex, an abbreviation for foreign exchange, is the market where currencies are traded. The exchange rate between two currencies is constantly changing, presenting opportunities for traders to profit from these small fluctuations. In forex trading, one currency is always exchanged for another, with the trader essentially buying one currency while selling another. For example, the EUR/USD pair represents the exchange rate of the euro against the US dollar. Although it may seem complex, the concept of trading one asset for another applies to all investments. When you purchase a share of Apple, you are essentially acquiring an AAPL/USD asset, indicating that you are betting on Apple's value rather than the US dollar's value.

One important note about currencies is that they tend to depreciate over time, primarily due to the continuous printing of money.

Cryptocurrencies

Cryptocurrencies, the pioneers of the digital financial era, are virtual currencies leveraging the power of cryptography for security. In stark contrast to traditional government-issued currencies such as the U.S. dollar or the euro, cryptocurrencies embrace decentralization, relying on blockchain technology for their operation. Emerging only within the last few decades, cryptocurrencies initially held a nominal value of almost $0, paving the way for remarkable value surges in recent times.

Despite their soaring performances, it's important to question the common perception that attracts enthusiasts. I believe 95% of individuals hold misconceptions about cryptocurrencies, often influenced by their impressive historical gains. When we see a price chart, we tend to forget what's behind.

You may think that my perception of cryptos is wrong as well. I have no problem with that. My personal philosophy in investing is and will always be, to invest in undervalued assets with increasing intrinsic values. Is Bitcoin the future? Maybe. But its intrinsic value is changing very little. If its intrinsic value remains quasi-constant, its worth is primarily driven by the increasing adoption of it.

We are nowadays at a point where people buy cryptocurrencies to earn money rather than using them for purchasing goods or services. If bitcoin is as good as it's claimed to be, why are we still conducting transactions in dollars? I don't see any compelling reason for governments to allow a decentralized means of purchasing. Instead, they are more likely to introduce their own crypto versions of the dollar and euro. However, these government-backed cryptocurrencies would likely exhibit a value trajectory similar to that of traditional currencies, with a volatility of 1 to 5% per year.

I don't see much strategic interest in specializing in cryptocurrencies in the long run. Moreover, the competition is extremely high in this space, as everyone seems to be drawn to them.

This section may present a somewhat negative perspective on cryptos. I emphasize that it is solely my point of view and you are free to make your own decisions. I would advise everyone to exercise caution when considering trading cryptocurrencies.

"It is unbelievable to witness that most people find cryptocurrencies and stocks even comparable."

- an old school man, me.

Commodities

Commodities are primary agricultural products or raw materials traded on exchanges, serving as the foundation for various economic goods and services. They are broadly categorized into two types: hard commodities and soft commodities.

Hard commodities

These are tangible, physical goods mined or extracted from the earth. Examples include:

- **Metals:** Gold, silver, copper.

- **Energy Resources:** Crude oil, natural gas, coal.

- **Agricultural Products:** Wheat, corn, soybeans.

Gold is the most popular commodity, often considered a safe haven, protecting wealth in difficult times. However, it's important to note that gold doesn't produce anything and has limited practical uses in our society. If you want to invest in gold, you can either buy physical gold or trade it in the financial market. While the financial market offers fewer guarantees to protect your gold, opting for physical gold may entail higher commissions.

Soft commodities

These commodities primarily consist of agricultural products and other consumables that are cultivated rather than extracted. Soft commodities are often perishable and serve as essential inputs in various industries. Examples include:

- **Agricultural Products:** Coffee, sugar, cotton.

- **Livestock:** Cattle, hogs.

- **Other Natural Resources:** Timber.

Alternative investments

Remember that there is, of course, a wide range of non-financial assets that can also be traded, such as:

- Art

- Collectibles: rare coins, vintage cars, etc.

- Farmlands

- Wines

- Watches

My personal recommendation is to focus on trading stocks and bonds. As mentioned previously, these assets are meant to generate profits, unlike most other assets. However, other assets can be used to diversify your investment portfolio or safeguard your wealth. The best choice for you also depends on your talents and knowledge.

Inflation

You are likely familiar with the concept of inflation. It refers to the decrease in the value of money over time. In simpler terms, it means that as time passes, you require more money to purchase the same things. Inflation is a common occurrence and has a direct impact on our everyday lives.

"You can be invincible if you avoid fights whose outcome is out of your control."

- Epictetus

So to the question "how to shield ourselves from the effects of inflation?". The answer is straightforward: "no money".

All non-monetary assets are immune to the erosive effects of inflation. Money has no impact on the intrinsic value of these assets. Consequently, their prices will move in the opposite direction of the value of money. All the assets seen previously except forex and bonds are often resilient to inflation.

One of the worst sentence I heard in my career is "Cash is king". In reality, the accurate statement should be "Cash makes me loose on average 2% every year" and "Value is king". Cash is just a means to exchange value.

Beyond inflation, there is depreciation, but again, it is all about value. Some possessions naturally decrease in value over time. Two examples of such assets are cars and products closely associated with technology. In simpler terms, certain things become less valuable on their own as time passes. This devaluation occurs without any external influence, making it a part of the inherent nature of these assets.

In conclusion, it's important to avoid holding large amounts of cash over an extended period and making purchases that have a strong natural depreciation. Keep in mind these two different concepts.

The opposite of inflation is deflation, where money's value increases. This event is usually more detrimental to the economy but also rarer, as all governments try to avoid it.

Styles of trading

There are three main styles of trading in the financial market:

- Scalping: This involves holding positions for a short period, typically a few minutes.

- Day trading: This involves holding a position for a single day or less. Day traders are more focused on price movements during a single trading session and aim to close their positions before the end of the day.

- Swing trading: This involves holding a position for several days, weeks, or even months. Swing traders aim to capture medium-term price movements and are less concerned with short-term fluctuations.

As for positions held for years, we usually talk about investment rather than trading.

Each style of trading has its own benefits and drawbacks. Scalping can be highly profitable, but it's also extremely stressful and requires constant attention. Day trading is less stressful than scalping but still requires a lot of focus and discipline. Swing trading is less demanding and provides traders with additional time to analyze the markets, but requires more patience and a longer-term perspective.

It is not stated that a scalper will generate greater profits than a swing trader.

It's important to note that different trading styles may lead to opposite predictions, but both can be right on their own timeframe. You must find a style that suits your situation, personality and risk tolerance. Overall, it's advisable for beginners to avoid scalping and start with swing trading, as it offers a less stressful approach and more time for analysis. This approach should also reduce your losing trades as you will benefit from the natural market growth. Passive approaches, such as long-term investing, can also be highly effective for those who prefer a more hands-off approach to the markets; in this case, focus on ETFs.

How to trade?

Analyze charts

Analyzing charts is an essential aspect of trading, aiding investors in making informed decisions regarding the buying and selling of financial assets. With technological advancements, several tools are now available to facilitate easy and quick chart analysis. The final section of this book will guide you through the process of chart analysis.

One of the most popular and widely used charting tools is TradingView. It proves to be an excellent tool for investors seeking a quick and easy analysis of financial assets. With its extensive range of features and user-friendly interface, TradingView has emerged as one of the most favored charting tools in the world of trading.

Broker

Now, let's get to the point. In order to buy and sell financial assets, you'll need a broker. A broker is an individual or company that executes orders on the market on your behalf. Interactive Brokers stands out as a popular choice with low fees and a good level of security.

If you opt for a different broker, conduct thorough research to choose one that is reputable, safe and transparent with its fees – this is crucial. Additionally, try to steer clear of brokers that are heavily advertised, as they often have hidden fees. Personally, I have no better recommendation than Interactive Brokers.

Once your account is set up, you'll need to find the symbol for the asset you want to trade and place your order. In trading, we often use symbols rather than full names, so familiarizing yourself with the symbols of the assets you're interested in (Apple: AAPL, Microsoft: MSFT, etc.) is essential.

Types of orders

Once you have analyzed an asset (which will be covered in future chapters) and made a decision, you will need to know what type of order you want to place on your brokerage account.

For a better understanding of the following types of orders, they will be explained in a buying situation only. The opposite will be the case if you decide to sell instead.

Market order

The market order is the simplest and most likely the one you'll want to use. It is executed at the lowest available current price. With this order, you do not specify the price at which you want to buy; instead, you only indicate the number of shares you wish to purchase. It can be roughly considered as an immediate order.

Buy now

Limit order

A limit order is an order where you specify the maximum price you are willing to pay per share, along with the number of shares you want to purchase. This order will be automatically executed if the market price reaches or falls below the limit price you set.

Buy if it gets here or below

If the price remains at the limit you specified for only a short period, it's possible that your order will be partially filled, meaning you'll receive fewer shares than requested. In such cases, the remaining portion of your order will stay active until fully filled. This scenario is relatively rare and typically occurs with large capital orders or when trading assets with low liquidity.

Stop order

A stop order is essentially a market order that activates once the price reaches the minimum amount you are willing to pay per share. Unlike a limit order, the stop order level is positioned between the current market price and the direction you desire.

Buy in market order once it gets here

Take-profit and stop-loss

When it comes to exiting trades, one of the most important tools available to traders are stop-losses and take-profits. These tools allow traders to set specific price points at which they will automatically sell their positions, either to limit potential losses or secure profits.

Stop-losses are designed to limit the amount of money that can be lost on a trade. Traders can set a stop-loss order at a specific price point, below the current market price, to sell their position if the market price falls to that level. This can be helpful in preventing significant losses in the event that the market moves against the trader's position. For example, let's say a trader buys a stock at $84 and sets a stop-loss order at $74. If the stock's price falls to $74, the stop-loss order will trigger and automatically sell the position, limiting the loss to $10 per share.

On the other hand, a take-profit order is used to automatically sell a position when it reaches a predetermined price level, allowing traders to secure profits. This order is designed to lock in gains. Traders can set a take-profit order at a specific price point above the current market price. Once the market reaches or surpasses this predefined level, the take-profit order is triggered and the position is automatically sold.

Stop-loss at 74 and take-profit at 100

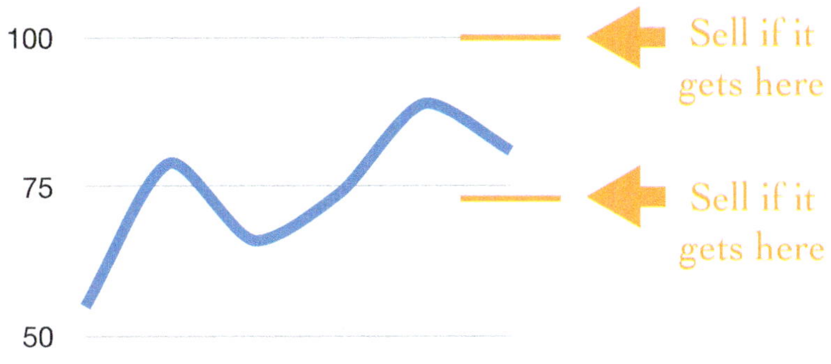
100
75
50
Sell if it gets here
Sell if it gets here

It's important to note that stop-loss and take-profit orders are not foolproof and can still result in losses or missed opportunities. The opening price of stocks can vary widely from the last close and the "best available price" in this case can be far from the level you initially set.

Additionally, professionals and institutions often try to anticipate where most traders have placed their stop-loss orders, with the intention of triggering them on purpose. This is known as "stop hunting". You must therefore place your level cautiously and with a bit of margin.

GTC and GFD

When placing your order, you will likely encounter the options "GTC" and "GFD". These terms pertain to the duration of an order.

GTC stands for "Good Till Cancelled". A GTC order stays active until the trader decides to cancel it or until it gets executed. On the other hand, GFD stands for "Good for Day". A GFD order remains active only for the current trading day. If the order is not filled by the end of the trading day, it will be automatically canceled.

Short selling

As mentioned earlier, it is also possible to speculate on a decline by selling before buying – holding a negative position.

Short selling is a trading strategy that involves selling an asset you currently don't own, with the aim of buying it back at a lower price in the future. While short selling can be a profitable way to speculate on a decline, it can also be very risky.

It's crucial to note that short selling comes with unlimited risk. Unlike buying, where the maximum loss is limited to the amount you invested (reached when the price is $0.00), short selling can result in significant losses as the asset's price continues to rise infinitely. For this reason, short selling is generally not recommended for beginners.

Furthermore, short selling goes against the general trend of the market, which is usually upward. As a result, it's essential to have a good understanding of the market and accurately predict changes in price direction before attempting to short sell.

Who owns stocks?

The wealthiest Americans dominate the stock market

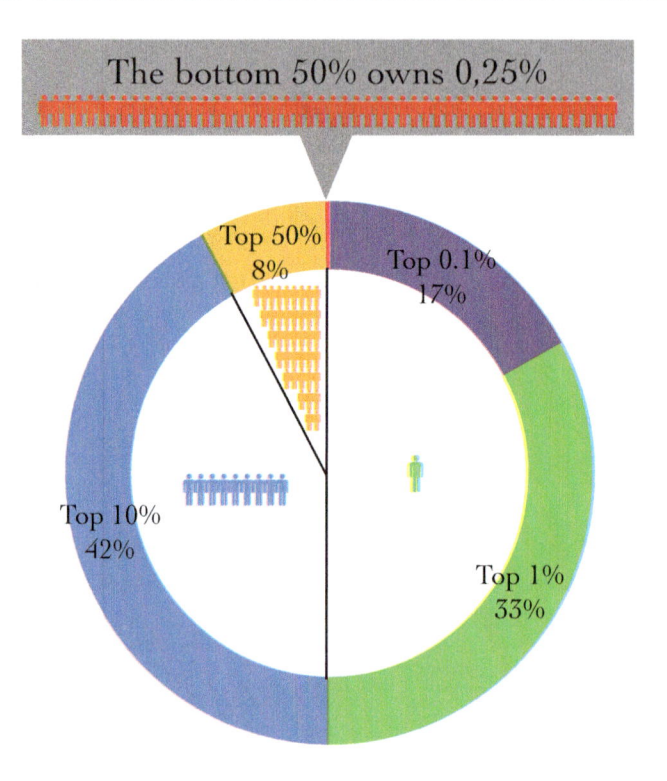

The bottom 50% owns 0,25%

Top 50%
8%

Top 0.1%
17%

Top 10%
42%

Top 1%
33%

Approximately 50% of the stock market is determined by only 1% of individuals, with the top 10% controlling 92%. This means that as a trader, you're mostly trading against these wealthy individuals.

The top 0.1% individuals are often referred to as the "whales" or "big boys" in the industry. However, despite their significant wealth, they face a unique challenge when trading. Their orders are often too large and buying everything at once could cause the price to skyrocket. As a result, they have to be strategic about how they place their orders to avoid driving the price up and ensure that they can execute their trades effectively. There's an opportunity to learn from them by observing their buying and selling patterns. Indeed, some uncommon big moves on the chart can sometimes unveil their intentions.

Risk and uncertainty

In life, when we refer to a situation as "risky", it typically implies a negative connotation. However, in finance, risk can manifest as either a detriment or a benefit. It's also important to understand the distinction between risk and uncertainty. Risk is quantifiable and can be expressed in terms of probabilities, while uncertainty lacks the information needed to gauge the likelihood of each outcome.

Decision-making with risk

When making financial decisions, a valuable tool at your disposal is the concept of the "lottery". It's a fundamental way of framing an investment as a game of chance with different possible results. To evaluate potential outcomes, we can represent various scenarios, their associated results and, if available, their probabilities.

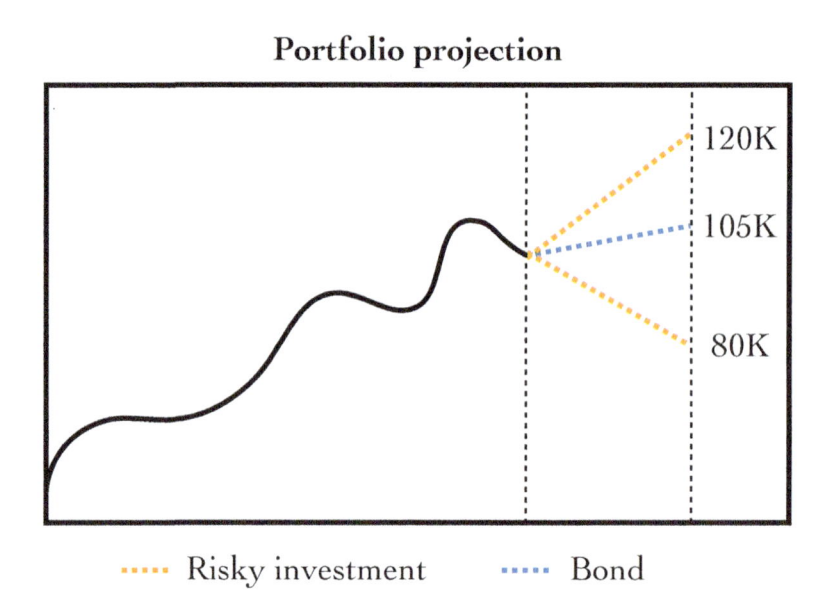

Portfolio projection

- - - - Risky investment   - - - - Bond

120K
105K
80K

In a conventional approach, when probabilities are known, we simply calculate the Expected Value (EV). It's the sum of each possible outcome multiplied by their probability.

For example, let's set a 70% probability of success for the risky investment.

Safe EV:
100% × 105K = 105K

Risky EV:
70% × 120K + 30% × 80K = 108K

In this case, the risky investment is the preferred choice if we are not overly concerned about volatility.

Here's an interesting point: with only one attempt, some may prefer the safe path out of fear of losing. However, if the lottery allows for a large amount of repetitions, mathematics tells us to consistently choose the option with the highest EV when positive, whether it's the risky one or not.

In trading, determining probabilities isn't always straightforward, which makes it challenging to ascertain the option with the highest EV. Nevertheless, the key takeaway is recognizing that life offers multiple opportunities. If you excel at identifying optimal EVs, risks become less significant, as mathematics proves long-term gains.

Going further, we can reverse the calculation to determine when the risky investment is no longer favorable. This is referred to as the "risk-neutral probability" or "risk-neutral measure".

Let's set up the equation "Risky EV = Safe EV" with "p" as the unknown variable representing the probability associated with the risky investment.

We have:

p × 120K + (1-p) × 80K = 105K

<=> 120Kp + 80K - 80Kp = 105K

<=> 40Kp = 25K

<=> p = 0.625

By performing this calculation, we eliminate the need to make a subjective prediction about the probability. The result becomes objective.

In conclusion, if we estimate that the probability of the risky investment reaching $120,000 exceeds 62.5%, then, according to this approach, the risky investment becomes more favorable as its Expected Value (EV) will surpass that of the safe investment.

This simplistic method allows traders to make decisions based on quantifiable data, reducing subjectivity and enhancing the precision of their choices in the face of risk.

Decision-making with uncertainty

In uncertain situations, where probabilities are unknown, calculating the Expected Value (EV) becomes unfeasible. Nevertheless, investors have alternative methods at their disposal to navigate such circumstances. The choice of approach depends on the investor's preferences and risk tolerance.

Here are a few of these methods:

Maximax

The Maximax strategy embodies optimism and is tailored for risk-tolerant investors. Essentially, this approach fervently selects the alternative with the highest potential payoff, emphasizing the best-case scenario. Assets aligned with this strategy often include cryptocurrencies, highly volatile stocks or leveraged ETFs.

Maximin

Conversely, the Maximin strategy adopts a conservative stance. In this approach, the decision-maker opts for the alternative that offers the maximum payoff in the worst-case scenario. This method prioritizes the minimization of potential losses or downside risk over the pursuit of aggressive gains. Assets typically associated with this strategy include gold and bonds.

Minimax Regret

The Minimax Regret strategy seeks to mitigate the "regret" associated with a decision. Regret is the disparity between the best conceivable outcome and the actual outcome achieved. In this approach, decision-makers evaluate various alternatives and select the one that minimizes the maximum regret. It serves as a means to account for the potential disappointment or remorse stemming from not choosing the optimal outcome.

While these concepts are undoubtedly highly theoretical, articulating your chosen approach and the ability to explain your decisions are indispensable for gaining profound insights into your personal decision-making process. Are you acting out of greed? Are you seeking to minimize regret? Are you prioritizing the safety of your wealth? Have an introspection and understand your motivations behind each decision.

Vocabulary

Finance's vocabulary is very wide and unique. Here are the most basic ones you'll need before we delve into the core of trading.

Financial asset:

Resource that has financial value and is expected to provide future economic benefits to its owner. Financial assets are intangible assets such as stocks, bonds, options, futures contracts and other derivatives, as well as cash and cash equivalents.

Being long:

Owning, betting on an increase in value.

Being short:

Selling, betting on a decrease in value.

Bear:

An investor who expects a decline in the market.

Bull:
An investor who expects prices to rise.

Bull market:
A market condition where prices are generally rising.

Bear market:
A market condition where prices are generally falling.

Diversification:
Owning a wide variety of assets to reduce the overall risk of your portfolio.

Dividend:
A payment made by a company to its shareholders, usually as a portion of profits.

IPO:
Initial Public Offering - the first time a company offers shares in the stock market.

Leverage or margin:
The use of borrowed money to increase potential returns.

Market capitalization:

The number of shares outstanding multiplied by the price of the shares. In short, it's the total amount invested in the company's shares.

Noise:

Refers to volatility that is not related to a specific current timeframe but to a higher one. We talk about noise when false signals are made in small timeframes by big long-term orders.

Pip:

Equivalent to 0.0001 points in the price. This metric is mostly used in forex, as currency prices are often close.

Portfolio:

A collection of all the current positions of a trader.

Reversal:

A change in the trend of the market.

Safe havens:

Assets supposed to retain or increase their value during market downturns.

Strategy:

A list of rules and criteria defining when to buy and when to sell.

Swing high/ Swing low:

Points on a price chart that indicate significant turning points. Local maximums and local minimums.

Timeframe:

A specified duration in which we analyze the chart: monthly, weekly, daily, 4 hours, etc.

Volatility:

The intensity of price fluctuations.

An upcoming rich:

You.

Second part
FUNDAMENTAL ANALYSIS

Fundamental analysis involves studying the company itself, examining factors such as its growth, revenue, projects, etc. This approach is primarily utilized for swing trading and long-term investing.

The price

A common mistake I've observed is people comparing stock prices and making decisions based on the apparent low price in dollars. This is a critical error that exposes a fundamental misunderstanding of what a stock truly represents.

The price of a stock is determined by two factors: the supply and the demand. The supply of a stock is the number of shares issued by the company, while demand is the total amount of money investors are willing to invest in the stock (the market capitalization).

$$\text{Price} = \frac{\text{Market Capitalization}}{\text{Number of Shares Outstanding}}$$

Therefore, just because Company A has a lower share price than Company B does not mean it is a better investment nor that it is a smaller company. It all depends on how many shares each company has issued.

It is even more concerning to witness some professional analysts, who are responsible for composing the world's leading ETFs, such as the Dow Jones Industrial Average, using price-weighted compositions. In price-weighted compositions, stocks with higher prices are assigned greater weight within the index. Consequently, stock splits, stock dividends and stock repurchases shift the weight distribution of the entire index with no fundamental reason. This is why I don't trust the DJIA as a reliable investment.

Due to this flaw, a company included in the DJIA can ascend to the top 1 in weight in the ETF simply by executing a reverse stock split, which is purely illogical.

It is better to consider other indexes, such as market-cap-weighted indices or broader benchmarks like the S&P 500, which take into account factors beyond just stock price (which means nothing) when it comes to weighting. These indices can be considered more logical, reliable and balanced.

Value & Growth

One of the most basic concepts of investing is the distinction between value and growth investing. Understanding the difference between the two can help you differentiate stocks and make better investment decisions.

Value investing

Value investing is a strategy that entails purchasing stocks undervalued by the market. The goal is to unearth stocks trading below their intrinsic value, determined by factors such as earnings, dividends, book value and cash flow.

Value investors believe that the market sometimes overreacts to short-term events and that good companies will eventually return to their intrinsic value (the proper value). Therefore, they seek stocks trading at a discount compared to their calculated intrinsic value.

To identify undervalued stocks, value investors employ various metrics, such as the price-to-earnings ratio (P/E) and the price-to-book ratio (P/B). We will delve deeper into these metrics later in this chapter. They help compare a company's valuation to its peers and the overall market.

Value investing requires patience and discipline. Investors must be willing to hold onto their positions for the long term, as it may take time for the market to recognize the true value of the stock.

Growth investing

Growth investing is a strategy that involves buying stocks that are expected to grow at a faster rate than the overall market. The goal is to find companies that have strong earnings growth potential and are expected to generate significant returns.

Growth investors typically seek companies that are industry leaders, possess a competitive advantage, undertake promising projects and have a solid management team. They also consider factors such as revenue growth, earnings growth and market share.

To identify growth stocks, investors use metrics such as earnings per share (EPS) growth rate, price-to-earnings-to-growth ratio (PEG) and price-to-sales ratio (P/S).

Growth investing requires a tolerance for risk, as growth stocks can be volatile and subject to sudden price swings. Investors must be willing to accept short-term fluctuations in the value of their holdings in exchange for the potential for long-term growth.

Value vs. Growth investing

Let's review both value and growth investing advantages and disadvantages:

- Value investing can provide a margin of safety, as it involves buying stocks that are trading at a discount to their intrinsic value. However, it may require patience and discipline to hold onto positions for the long term.

- Growth investing can provide the potential for significant returns, as it involves investing in companies with strong earnings growth potential.

However, it can also be risky, as growth stocks can be volatile and subject to sudden price swings.

It's important to note that value and growth are not mutually exclusive. Some companies may have both value and growth characteristics. Therefore, investors may choose to use a combination of both strategies when selecting stocks. They may also choose to own both value and growth stocks in order to diversify their portfolio. Understanding the difference between the two can help you make better investment decisions.

The book value

This section is in my opinion the second most important one of this book; the first being the section about compound interests.

One of the greatest ways to determine whether a company is priced fairly is by examining its book value.

Let's delve into the concept of book value through a practical example. Imagine you are the proprietor of an innovative company with a promising future. The collective worth of all your factories and stores amounts to $1 million. However, given the company's bright growth prospects, you might be able to sell it for a price exceeding $1 million.

Herein lies the distinction: the price of a company's ownership does not equate to the total value of everything the company possesses. The book value represents the sum of all a company's assets, inclusive of its debts (assets minus liabilities). In simpler terms, it's the total worth of everything the company owns when each component is assessed separately.

Price-to-book ratio

The price-to-book ratio compares a company's market value to its book value. By analyzing the price-to-book ratio, you can gain insight into whether a company is undervalued or overvalued in the market.

$$\text{PB ratio} = \frac{\text{Price of one share} \times \text{shares outstanding}}{\text{Assets} - \text{liabilities}}$$

$$\text{PB ratio} = \frac{\text{Market value}}{\text{Real value}}$$

A PB ratio of 1.2 means that the share's price is 20% above its book value, which represents the company's real value.

This ratio can easily be found on TradingView.

16.48

This ratio often fluctuates within clearly definable levels, facilitating market timing. However, it doesn't directly incorporate expected growth. A higher expected growth rate inevitably leads to a higher PB ratio, meaning that growth stocks tend to have higher PB ratios.

As of the time of writing this book, the price of a share of Ferrari is currently 16.48 times its book value, which is exceptionally high. Buyers are indeed paying significantly more than the company's real worth. This indicates a very positive sentiment from investors and a belief that the company will continue to grow.

Generally, high PB ratios should be approached with caution. For instance, Apple's PB ratio is currently over 40, indicating that it is 40 times more expensive than its real value. Despite recognizing the significant growth potential of this company, it's advisable to exercise caution. It is important to understand that some of the filters traders use when selecting companies are based on principles. This means that just because we reject Apple from our list, it doesn't imply that we believe it will not perform well. Rather, it is a matter of principle not to invest in companies that are 40 times overpriced. In summary, while Apple could continue to perform well in the coming years, its extremely high PB ratio suggests the potential for a significant drop and still be on a logical price.

The price-to-book (PB) ratio is one of my favorite indicators because it helps to stay grounded and not get carried away by overly bullish technical analysis. When the PB ratio is high, I become more cautious about buying, even if the technicals are strong. Of course, exclusively buying stocks with low PB ratios can be too restrictive and cause you to miss out on opportunities for high-growth stocks like Apple. However, sticking to low PB ratio stocks can significantly reduce your risk, provide a sense of safety in markets and help you compare similar stocks.

Book value per share

The book value per share is a useful measure that offers a more visual representation of a company's true value. To calculate the book value per share, simply divide the book value of the company by the total number of outstanding shares.

$$\text{Book value per share} = \frac{\text{Assets - liabilities}}{\text{Shares outstanding}}$$

Book value/share
(real value of the company)

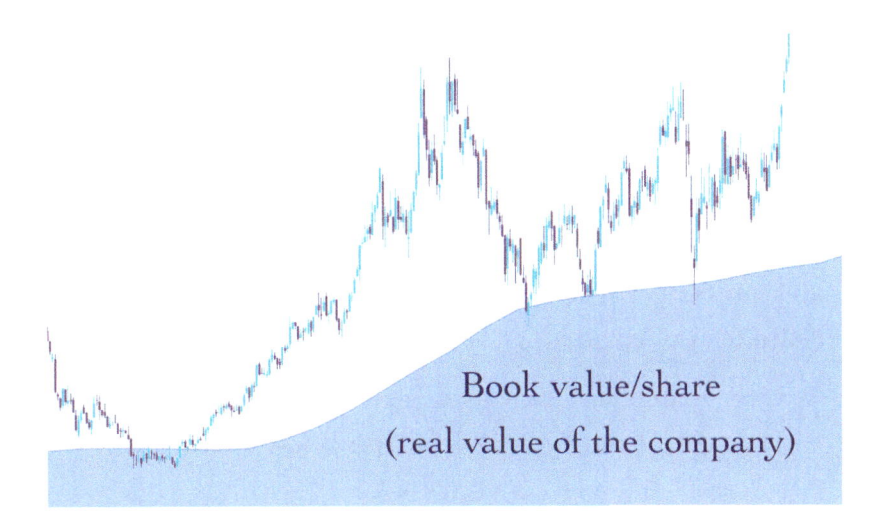

Of course, both the book value per share and the P/B ratio provide similar information. However, incorporating the book value per share into the price chart enhances the visual comparison of these values and clearly illustrates the growth of the book value over time. Additionally, as you can see, it often serves as a strong support level in some cases.

I truly believe that the study of the book value is underrated; it is better than focusing solely on revenue, income, EBITA, EBITBA, as it integrates them.

I also like to analyze the average book value evolution in the last 3 to 5 years and compare it to the price's one. Meaning that I try to find book values that have grown significantly in recent years as compared to the price.

As the growth is supposed to justify decorrelations between the market value and the book value, we can combine these 2 elements. For instance, we can create a new ratio:

$$\frac{\text{Average annual growth of the book value from 3 years} \times C}{\text{Price-to-book ratio}}$$

C being a constant that enables you to weigh the importance of both values as desired.

Now let's get to the very practical explanations. When it comes to the book value, I tend to search for stocks:

- member of the S&P 500 (or similar)

- with a low PB ratio as compared to the book value's growth

- with a continuous growth of the book value

- having an annual average book value's growth above 30% over the past 3-5 year's.

- having an annual average price growth below 20% over the past 3-5 year's.

In summary, all we try to compare is the book value's growth against the PB ratio and additionally, we need a consistent growth of the book value for safety.

Below is an example of a preferred situation concerning the book value.

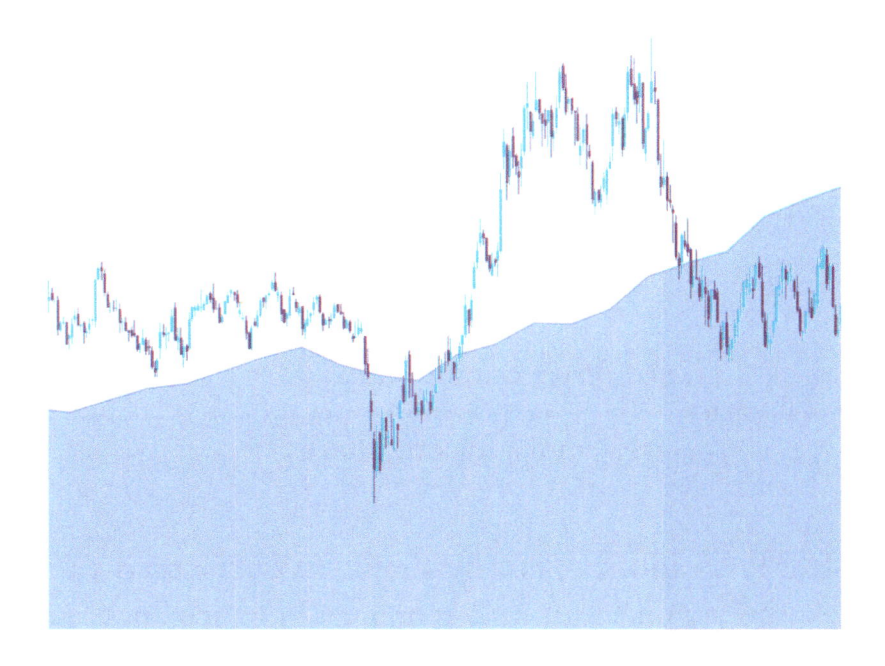

P/E ratio

You may have encountered the P/E ratio, one of the most widely used financial metrics in stock analysis. In simple terms, it represents the ratio of a company's stock price to its earnings per share (EPS) over a specific period. This metric is frequently employed to assess the relative value of a stock and compare it with other companies in the same industry or market.

A high P/E ratio often suggests that investors are willing to pay a premium for the company's earnings potential, while a low P/E ratio may indicate undervaluation or subdued growth prospects.

$$\text{P/E ratio} = \frac{\text{Price of one share}}{\text{Company's earnings / shares outstanding}}$$

$$\text{P/E ratio} = \frac{\text{Price of one share}}{\text{Earnings for one share}}$$

The P/E ratio is relatively simple to understand and can be summarized in 2 sentences. For instance, to interpret a P/E ratio of 16 we can say:

- For every $16 invested in the company, it generates $1 in earnings per year.

- It is currently taking 16 years for the company to generate earnings equivalent to the amount invested in it.

The most commonly recommended P/E ratio is below 17. Yet, akin to the PB ratio, a company's growth prospects wield a profound influence over its P/E ratio. Hence, it's not advisable to have strict rules for this ratio and it should be balanced with the company's growth potential.

This juncture births the PEG ratio, it represents the P/E ratio divided by the next year's projected earning growth.

The lower the PEG ratio, the more enticing is the stock.

	PE ratio	PEG ratio
Calculation	Price / earning per share	PE ratio / expected growth in 5 years
Ferrari	52	3.0
Tesla	71	1.2

In the example, Ferrari appears less overpriced than Tesla based on the P/E ratio. However, when considering the projected growth, Tesla becomes much more interesting. The expected growth is, of course, a highly debatable metric that will vary from one analyst to another.

This revision makes the sequence of ideas clearer and refines the expression of the comparison

Piotroski score

One useful and straightforward tool in fundamental analysis is the Piotroski Score, named after its creator, Joseph Piotroski. It is a metric that assesses a company's financial health based on specific accounting metrics. The score ranges from 0 to 9, with higher scores indicating stronger financial performance. Traders and investors use the score to identify companies that are financially stable and have strong prospects for future growth. The score consists of nine accounting-based measures, each of which receives a point if it meets certain criteria. These criteria are based on the financial statements of the company and include factors such as profitability, asset quality and financial leverage.

The nine criteria are:

1. Positive net income

2. Positive operating cash flow

3. Higher return on assets (ROA) compared to the previous year

4. Cash flow from operations is greater than net income

5. Lower long-term debt to assets ratio compared to the previous year

6. Higher current ratio compared to the previous year

7. No new shares issued in the previous year

8. Gross margin improved compared to the previous year

9. Higher asset turnover compared to the previous year

Each criterion that is met is awarded a point, while criteria that are not met receive zero points. The total number of points is then added up to give the score for that particular company. This score can also be found on TradingView.

Companies that score 8 or 9 are considered financially strong and are more likely to have good prospects for future growth.

Conversely, companies with a score of 0 to 2 are considered weak and may be at high risk of financial distress.

The Piotroski score can be used in a number of ways to inform investment decisions. For example, it can be used as a filter to screen out weak companies from a list of potential investments. It can also be used as a tool to identify undervalued companies with strong financials that may be trading at a discount to their true value.

The fundamental analysis that no one talks about

Beyond this multitude of ratios and metrics, what most investors tend to forget are the non-measurable elements of the company. Figures cannot define a company's future in its entirety.

Think of Elon Musk. A well managed company, with unique expertise, with a great ability to find gaps in the market, that has proved its resilience in difficult times, may surpass those with superior ratios but lacking these characteristics.

Finding undervalued stocks is great, but don't forget quality. Forget about the ratios for some time, take a banknote of $100 in your hand and ask yourself: "Who in this world can take the most care of these $100?" and "Which company will bring the most value to the future?"

In conclusion of the fundamental analysis, as all companies are different, each data needs to be put in perspective. Additionally, all elements and all signs need to be positive. As an example, no matter how great ratios are, it would be a big mistake to invest if the Piotroski score is of 2 and conversely.

Third part
MANAGING TRADES

Risk management and money management are two closely related concepts and work together to support successful trading.

The goal of risk management is to protect your trading capital and prevent significant losses. This can include using stop-loss orders and diversifying your portfolio for example.

Money management, on the other hand, focuses on the management of the money that you are using to trade. This includes managing your trading capital, determining the appropriate position size and setting profit and loss targets. The goal of money management is to maximize your returns and minimize your losses by making the most efficient use of your trading capital.

One way to manage money is to use a technique called position sizing. Position sizing is the process of determining the appropriate number of shares or contracts to trade based on your trading capital.

This helps to ensure that you don't over-leverage your account and risk losing all of your capital.

Another way to manage money is to set profit and loss targets in order to have a good risk-reward ratio.

We roughly can simplify these concepts as follows:

Risk management = Diversification + Stop-loss

Money management = Sizing + Risk-reward ratio

Diversification

Diversification in trading can be seen as a strategy of heterogeneity, promoting plurality, spreading the capital in order to reduce the overall risk. Keep in mind that the risk can be both beneficial or detrimental. Therefore, diversification improves the resilience of your portfolio and typically increases the predictability of its performance, as board performances are less volatile than its components.

There are several types of diversification in trading. Below are the main ones from boarder to more specific order.

Geographic Diversification: Expanding investments into different continents or countries to reduce the risk from location-specific events. Continents tend to be poorly correlated.

Asset Class Diversification: Spreading investments across different asset classes: stocks, bonds, real estate, etc.

Sector Diversification: Investing in various sectors within a specific asset class: water, technology, healthcare, etc.

Time Horizon Diversification: Having investments based with different timeframes: day trading, swing trading, etc.

Risk Diversification: Allocating a portion of your portfolio to high risk and low risk.

Factor-Based Diversification: Focusing on specific factors like value, growth, dividends, etc.

Trading Strategy Diversification: Using various trading methods: strategy A, strategy B, strategy C.

Company or Stock Diversification: Holding shares in multiple companies to mitigate risk associated with individual company performance.

Etc.

Many of these types of diversification can be achieved through ETFs, for instance. It's important to note that diversification does not eliminate risk entirely but aims to manage and reduce it. The appropriate diversification strategy will depend on your financial goals, risk tolerance and investment horizon. Diversification must take into account the correlation between assets; the more they are inversely correlated, the greater the diversification. It's also essential to regularly review and rebalance your portfolio to maintain your desired diversification levels as market conditions change.

I, nowadays, rely on very few diversifications, but this could be badly interpreted. You always need to have a portfolio you're comfortable with. Here are the sine qua non diversification rules for your long term success:

- Always have at least 30% of your money in the safest spots. This will be your emergency fund.

- The flow between the emergency fund and the rest is one-sided. In other words, money can only go into your emergency fund but never out. For instance, when the other 70% goes down, never use the emergency fund to fill it back. When the 70% goes up, send the additional money to the emergency fund to maintain the 30% threshold.

Asset classes

Let's take a closer look at asset class diversification. BlackRock provides a very useful map that shows the best-performing asset classes year by year. As you can see, U.S. equities have been by far the most profitable in recent years.

BlackRock Asset Return Map

2015	2016	2017	2018	2019	2020	2021	2022	2023	2024		Annualised
Japan equities 9.9%	High yield 14.3%	China equities 54.3%	Cash 1.9%	U.S. equities 31.6%	China equities 29.7%	Commodities 38.5%	Commodities 22%	U.S. equities 27.1%	Japan equities 4.6%		U.S. equities 12.5%
U.S. equities 1.3%	Infrastructure 12.4%	EM equities 37.8%	DM gov. debt -0.4%	Infrastructure 27%	U.S. equities 21.4%	REITs 32.5%	Cash 1.3%	Japan equities 20.8%	Commodities 3.8%		Japan equities 6.2%
Emerging debt 1.2%	U.S. equities 11.6%	Europe equities 26.2%	IG credit -3.5%	Europe equities 24.6%	EM equities 18.7%	U.S. equities 27%	Infrastructure -0.2%	Europe equities 20.7%	U.S. equities 1.6%		Infrastructure 5.5%
REITs 0.6%	EM equities 11.6%	Japan equities 24.4%	High yield -4.1%	REITs 24.5%	Japan equities 14.9%	Europe equities 17%	High yield -12.7%	High yield 14%	Cash 0.4%		REITs 5.2%
Cash 0.1%	Emerging debt 10.2%	U.S. equities 21.9%	U.S. equities -4.9%	China equities 23.7%	IG credit 10.1%	Infrastructure 11.9%	Europe equities -14.5%	REITs 11.5%	Europe equities -0.1%		Europe equities 5.1%
Europe equities -2.3%	Commodities 9.7%	Infrastructure 20.1%	Emerging debt -4.6%	Japan equities 20.1%	DM gov. debt 9.5%	Japan equities 2%	IG credit -16.1%	Emerging debt 10.5%	High yield -0.2%		High yield 3.6%
High yield -2.7%	REITs 6.9%	High yield 10.4%	REITs -4.8%	EM equities 18.9%	High yield 7%	High yield 1%	Japan equities -16.3%	EM equities 10.3%	IG credit -0.5%		EM equities 3.2%
DM gov. debt -3.3%	IG credit 6%	Emerging debt 9.3%	Infrastructure -9.6%	Emerging debt 14.4%	Europe equities 5.9%	Cash 0%	Emerging debt -16.5%	IG credit 10.2%	Emerging debt -1.2%		Emerging debt 3%
IG credit -3.8%	Japan equities 2.7%	IG credit 9.3%	Commodities -10.7%	High yield 12.6%	Emerging debt 5.9%	Emerging debt 1.5%	DM gov. debt -17.5%	Infrastructure 6.8%	DM gov. debt -1.9%		IG credit 1.9%
China equities -7.8%	DM gov. debt 1.7%	REITs 8.6%	Japan equities -12.6%	IG credit 11.8%	Cash 0.7%	IG credit -2.1%	U.S. equities -19.5%	Cash 5.1%	Infrastructure -3.1%		Cash 1.3%
Infrastructure -11.5%	China equities 1.1%	DM gov. debt 7.3%	EM equities -14.2%	Commodities 11.8%	Infrastructure -5.8%	EM equities -2.2%	EM equities -19.7%	DM gov. debt 4.2%	REITs -4%		Commodities 1%
EM equities -14.6%	Cash 0.4%	Commodities 1.7%	Europe equities -14.3%	DM gov. debt 5.6%	REITs -8.1%	DM gov. debt -6.6%	China equities -21.8%	Commodities 0%	EM equities 4.0%		China equities 0.6%
Commodities -23.0%	Europe equities 0.2%	Cash 0.8%	China equities -18.7%	Cash 2.3%	Commodities -9.3%	China equities -21.6%	REITs -23.6%	China equities -11%	China equities -10.6%		DM gov. debt -0.6%

Key: Lowest return ──────► highest return

Your strategy of investment should not depend on your total wealth but rather on the size of your savings as compared to it.

Case 1: Small wealth as compared to earnings

If your total wealth is smaller than your 2 years' savings (excluding trading), you can take more risks and diversify a little less because recovering from a loss would be easier for you. You could probably focus on the stock market only and maybe even allocate 5% to 15% in cryptocurrencies (although I don't like and don't recommend them, but everyone is different). This approach holds until you get to Case 2.

Case 2: Big wealth as compared to earnings

If the wealth you have could take more than 2 years to recover completely, you should definitely diversify more.

In any case, it is worth doing this calculation to keep in mind the answers to "In how many years could I recover all?"

Here's a portfolio that I would recommend to an average trader. Remember that you must be honest with yourself and recognize that aggressiveness can be tempting, but it also carries a higher risk of losses and volatility. Additionally, it's crucial to carefully select high-quality assets.

Bonds ■ **ETF** ■ **Stocks** ■ **Leveraged ETF**

⟵ Protective — Aggressive (and more active) ⟶

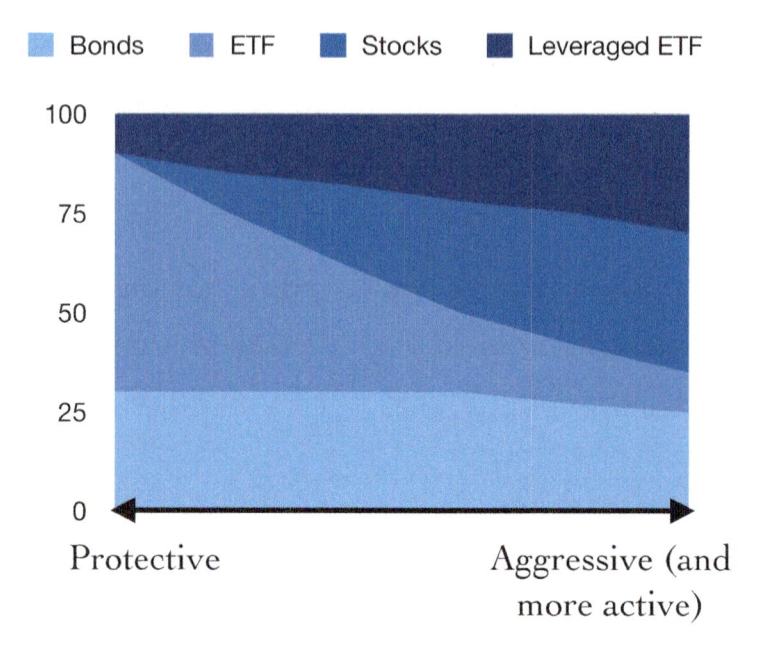

Beginners must, of course, start with a protective approach. The reason bonds occupy a more constant portion of the portfolio is their ability to reduce overall volatility and provide a sense of stability for the trader. Bonds are an attractive asset class that can contribute to maintaining a higher level of calm and tranquility within a portfolio. Moreover, they can be used as the 30% safety fund mentioned previously.

Lastly, each portion should be adapted to your current macro-market perspectives but also to the quality of stocks that you can find. For instance, if you don't find wonderful undervalued stocks in a certain period, then you could focus on ETFs.

Risk reward ratio

The risk-reward ratio is a very commonly used tool that compares the take-profit price to the stop-loss price. The take-profit price is the level at which you aim to close your order in a favorable scenario, while the stop-loss is the level in the unfortunate scenario. Regarding the break-even point, it is the level at which you initiated the order—neither gaining nor losing.

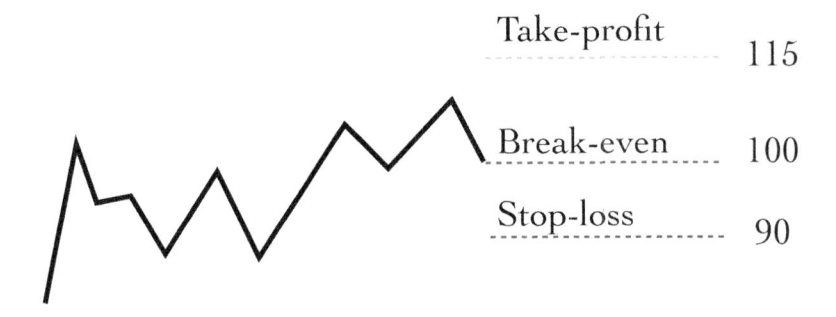

```
                    Take-profit      115
        /\                 
    /\ /  \  /\    Break-even    100
 /\/  V    \/  \                   
/              \   Stop-loss       90
```

In this example, our risk-reward ratio is 15/10 = 1.5, the aimed gain divided by the absolute value of the loss accepted.

Many influencers pretend that you simply need to have a high risk-reward ratio to earn money in trading, as you will earn more than you lose. However, this shows a lack of competence as they clearly ignore probabilities. Fundamental thinking gives the variation of your risk-reward ratio a neutral impact on profit. Indeed, the closer the level is to break-even, the higher the probability of reaching it in a given period. In essence, you should only adapt this ratio to your trading style and to each specific trade.

Getting rid of potential losses

According to this, how to be 100% sure you will not lose money on a trade?

The first way is not to trade.

The second is to put your stop-loss at break-even. By doing so, your maximum loss will be zero and your gains are unlimited. This approach can eliminate 80% of your fear, allowing you to trade with confidence and resist the urge to take profits too early.

To clarify, let the price move in your desired direction and as soon as it's sufficiently away from the level at which you bought, set the stop-loss at break-even or even above. This will only work if you were already making a profit at the time you set the stop-loss at break-even of course. The only exception would be a price opening directly under your wished level.

Example:

1 Placing order

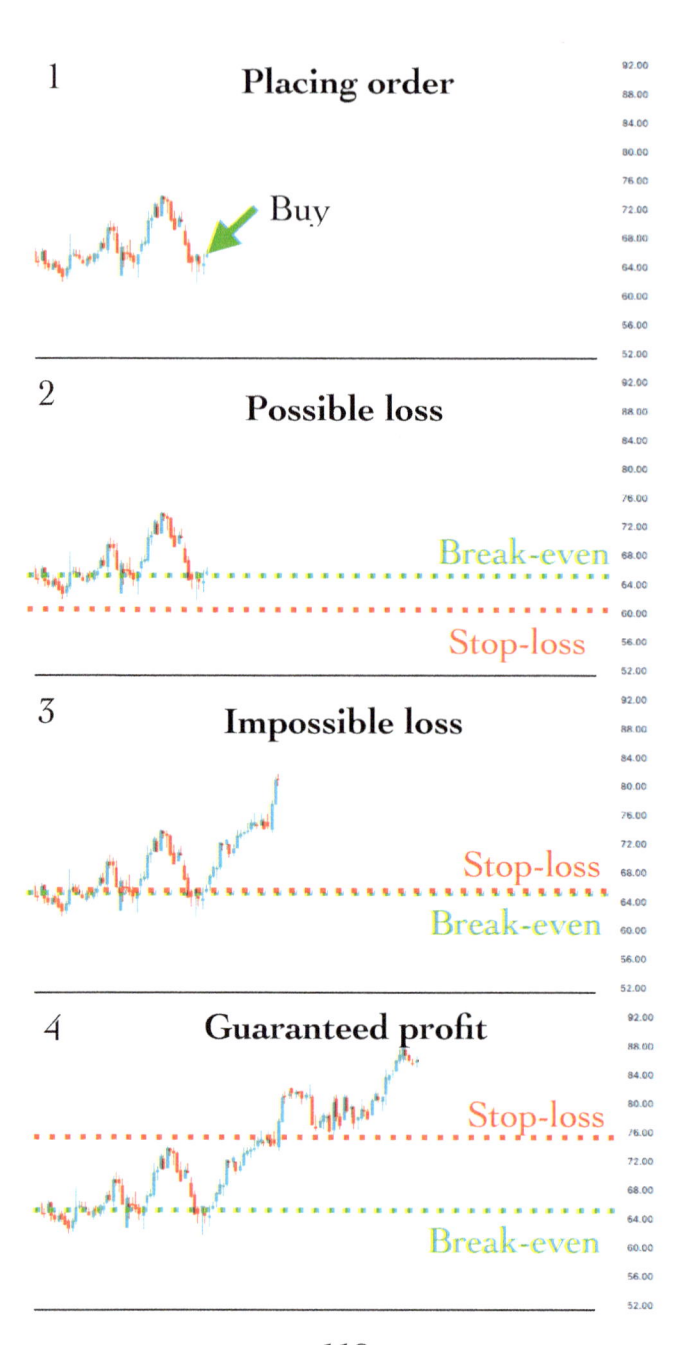

Buy

2 Possible loss

Break-even

Stop-loss

3 Impossible loss

Stop-loss

Break-even

4 Guaranteed profit

Stop-loss

Break-even

Lump-sum investing vs Dollar-cost averaging

Lump-sum investing (LSI) is the strategy of investing a large sum of money all at once, rather than spreading it out over time. This approach is commonly favored by investors confident in market conditions, enabling them to capitalize on the full potential of upcoming market movements.

On the other hand, dollar-cost averaging (DCA) is a more conservative investment strategy. It involves investing a fixed amount of money at regular intervals, regardless of market conditions. This method is often preferred by investors who harbor uncertainty about market perspectives, as it helps mitigate the risk of investing all their funds at an inopportune time.

LSI   **DCA**

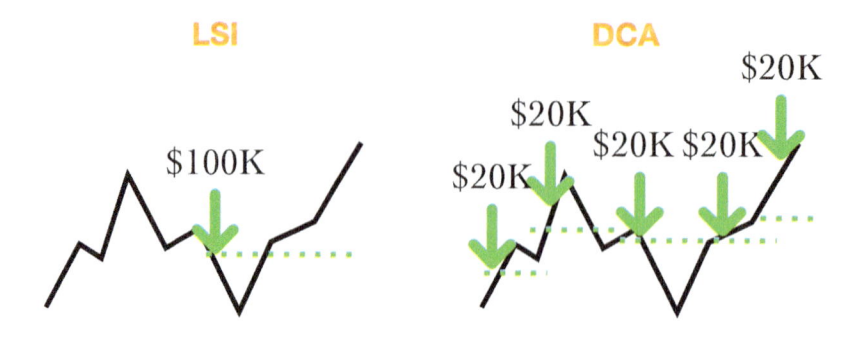

$100K $20K $20K $20K $20K $20K

• • • • Average total buying price

As these concepts are easy to understand, let's delve into further details. Both LSI and DCA have their pros and cons, and the strategy you choose will depend on your personal investment style, risk tolerance, time horizon of the trade and the significance of the amount to you. In the context of swing trading and investing, it's important to note that markets tend to grow over time. Therefore, smoothing your entry into the market with DCA will result in some non-invested money during the process.

Empirically, in the long term, it is roughly 2 out of 3 times better to invest all the money at once (LSI) rather than smoothing your entry into the market (DCA). The more spaced out the DCA is in time, the more its results underperform LSI (90% of the time when the DCA lasts 3 years).

So, reasoning according to performance, LSI has better probabilistic growth potential. However, as humans, most people might panic when faced with significant volatility in their wealth, especially with a large order. Investing all at once can be very stressful, potentially leading to regret or excessive fear, resulting in further poor trading choices.

I like to say that traders have three capitals: one is monetary, another is the amount of time they still have and the third one is emotional. Regarding the third, it is indeed important to find a balance that will not bring too much stress.

Mixed approach

In many cases, my personal recommendation is a hybrid approach that additionally takes into account the price. For instance, DCA and LSI can be done 50-50. We would have 50% of the capital all at once at first, then 50% smoothed with DCA. However, our implementation of the DCA would depend upon the price, meaning that I would not buy (or buy less than planned) if the price is above my LSI level.

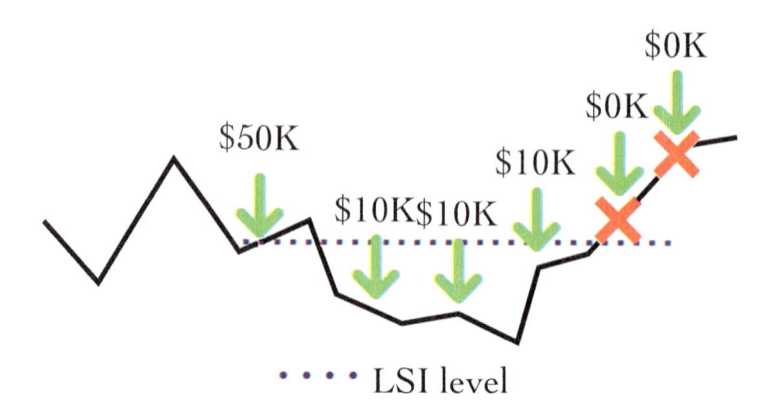

[Chart showing price movements with arrows: $50K, $10K, $10K, $10K, $0K, $0K marked along a price line with LSI level indicated by dotted line. Green down arrows indicate buys, orange X marks indicate skipped purchases above LSI level.]

• • • • LSI level

In this example, we want to make a $100K investment by putting 50% in LSI and 50% in DCA. However, we only do the DCA if the price is lower than the LSI level. In this case, we end up investing $80K rather than $100K. If indeed this technique might make the trader invest less than planned, it is extremely powerful when it comes to the serenity of the trader. Very few regrets will emerge from such a practice. If the price rises too fast, you will feel comfortable having at least put 50% of your desired money and if the price goes down, your fear will be lowered as you would still have 50% in reserve to invest in it.

Price & time approach

Another DCA method that I find particularly pertinent when it comes to very big orders is to split the investment not only according to the time going on but also to the current price.

In this case, we can draw a rectangle on the chart and divide this rectangle by a desired amount. You will need to define 3 elements:

- The last date X at which you want to be fully invested.

- The lowest price Y that could be reached in your opinion.

- Define if you want a hybrid approach or not. (Is it important to already be invested?)

Let's take an example of the amount of money to invest when we divide by 4, without a hybrid approach. Once a percentage is reached, it should not be lowered, of course, even if the price goes up.

Simple option (orthogonal):

	Start date				X
∞	0%	25%	50%	75%	100%
Start price	0%	25%	50%	75%	100%
1/4 away from Y	25%	25%	50%	75%	100%
1/2 away from Y	50%	50%	50%	75%	100%
3/4 away from Y	75%	75%	75%	75%	100%
Y	100%	100%	100%	100%	100%

Linear option:

	Start date				X
∞	0%	25%	50%	75%	100%
Start price	0%	25%	50%	75%	100%
1/4 away from Y	25%	50%	75%	100%	
1/2 away from Y	50%	75%	100%		
3/4 away from Y	75%	100%			
Y	100%				

It should simply be adapted to your preference.

In conclusion, we set a smoothing methodology combining the principles:

- Wanting to be fully invested if the price reaches Y.

- Wanting to be fully invested if the date reaches X.

This technique is more active than the previous ones as you will need to check the price regularly.

Do the opposite

In 1990, Peter Lynch reached his 13th year being at the head of the Fidelity Magellan fund. It averaged a 29.2% annual return, making it the most performing mutual fund in the world. It made roughly 28 times the initial investment in 13 years. You might think that the members were extremely lucky to belong to this fund. What if I said no?

According to Fidelity, the average investor lost money during those 13 years in this fund. Not because of fees, not because of a drop at the end, only because they were driven by their emotions. People were indeed doing the exact opposite of what they should.

"The stock market is the only market where customers run out of the store when there's a sale."

Most investors buy when high performances show up and sell in panic when they see their money go away. It sounds logical, but these are extremely poor investment decisions, making the average investor underperform the S&P 500.

However, it may reassure you to know that it does not only concern retail traders. People often tend to give a bad image of retail traders, but in reality, many studies have shown that about 90% of professionals underperform the S&P500. Meaning that buying it would bring you directly into the top 10% of professional traders.

People tend to think they are better than others, so they will outperform broad indexes. However, of course, it is possible; you can be part of the top 10%, but you need to stop reacting like everyone does. The rule is simple: as long as your own portfolio doesn't outperform indexes, buy indexes.

It is easy to earn money in trading. But you need to get rid of your emotions. It is when people lose all hope that it's time to buy. And when you think it can only go up, it is often time to sell.

In short, what's the moral of this? Focus on long-term performances, your indicators and the fundamentals; not on the recent -30% drop. Most traders lose money, just do the opposite. You won't be disappointed.

The emotion of the market

The best way to understand the market sentiment is by analyzing the price. The notion of "price" can seem very blurry and unclear to most people. You should think of it as the consensus, the average value given by investors.

Except from the study of the price from indexes, for example, there are four other elements I recommend checking to understand the consensus.

The VIX

The Volatility S&P500 index serves as a measure of the expected volatility of the American market. The higher it is, the more greedy investors are and the lower it is, the more scared they are.

VIX index

The Fear and Greed Index

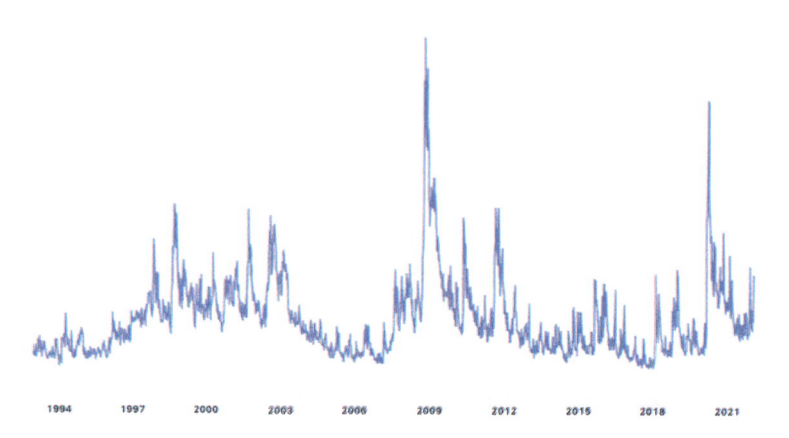

The Fear and Greed Index, it is my favorite; you won't find it in TradingView but on cnn.com. Below 10%-20%, you can consider it a long-term buy signal and a sell signal when it's above 80%-90%.

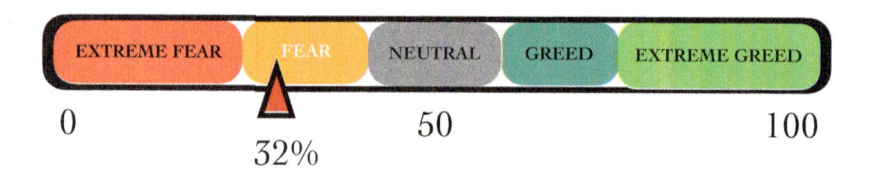

This measure takes into account various factors, including market volatility, stock price momentum, trading volumes, breadth of market participation, etc. Each factor is assigned a certain weight. It is, of course, not a perfect indication.

The DXY

The DXY The US Dollar Index (DXY) is a measure of the value of the US dollar relative to a basket of six foreign currencies: the euro, the Japanese yen, the British pound, the Canadian dollar, the Swedish krona and the Swiss franc. Introduced in 1973, it has since become an important indicator of the strength of the US dollar in the global market. It also gives insight on the amount of cash people have. Remember, if you buy Apples's stocks, for instance, you are betting on and "AAPL/USD" - Apple's stock against the US dollar. A high DXY can be an indication to buy.

The medias

By "media", I'm not referring to being informed every day and watching the news. Nonetheless, the more bullish content you see on an asset, the more likely it is to drop. People tend to become bullish when the price has already soared significantly.

Bitcoin's price vs subscribers of a random influencer in cryptocurrencies

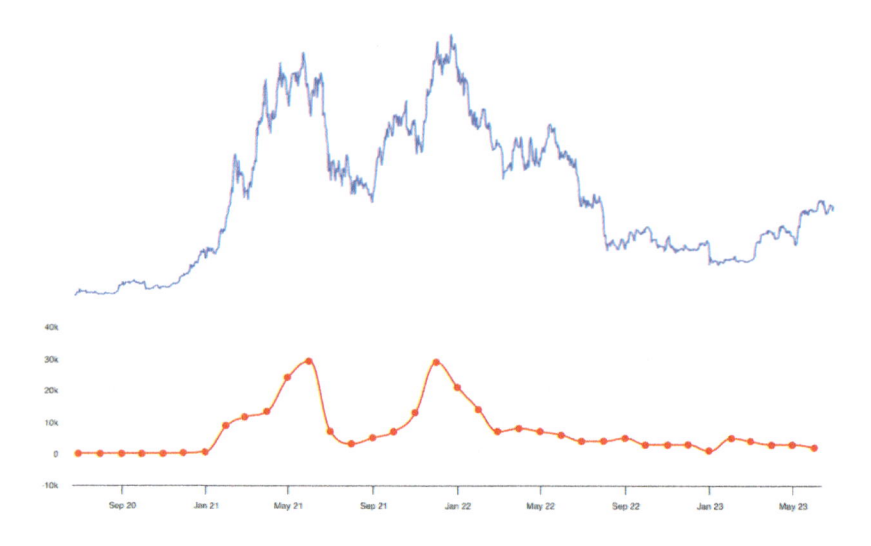

Missing the train

In trading, if you wanted to buy an asset but the price went too high before you knew it, you should probably not buy it. If you childishly start to run behind the train, not only will you not attain it, but you might also miss the next one. Even though it's hard, if you missed it, you should better wait for the next train.

There is no one best way

One important aspect of trading is that there's no one best way to trade. Numerous paths can lead to the same outcome, meaning there are numerous strategies that can yield wealth. For instance, some individuals choose to rebalance their portfolio on a weekly or monthly basis, allocating recent gains to assets that have gone down. Conversely, the opposite approach appears equally logical, as it involves allocating more resources to the best-performing assets. Therefore, you must find approaches that align with your personal style. As you gain experience in trading, you will gradually develop your own unique path.

Margins

We've already discussed leveraged ETFs at the beginning of this book. Margins are similar, but in this case, you will need to borrow money. Nowadays, it is possible to borrow money directly from your broker (with its own interest rate).

If you have a $1000 account and borrow $2000 from your broker, your margin rate is 3000/1000 = 3. In this case, your normal trading performances are multiplied by 3. Despite the attractiveness of margins, they should not be used by beginners.

In the previous case, if your $1000 lost 34% of its value, you would be liquidated, which means you would end up with $0, with no way to recover that money back.

To calculate the maximum loss your trade can have by using margins, you simply have to divide -1 by your margin rate. In this example, it's -1/3 = -0.3333 = -33.33% of maximal loss before liquidation.

Understanding how this system works is crucial to avoid mistakes. In the previous example, the $2000 you borrow are fixed, but your $1000 will vary three times more. This affects your margin rate in an undesired way. For instance, let's say your investment goes down 20%; you would still be borrowing $2000, but you would only own $400, giving a new margin rate of 2400/400 = 6, which is very risky.

My recommendation is to never borrow more than 40% of your own money, resulting in a 1.4 margin rate. It should also align with the diversification and safety of your portfolio. For example, I can have

100% invested in the stock market and 25% in bonds for which I borrow money.

Protecting your account

It's common for beginners to experience substantial losses and many traders end up depleting the funds of their initial trading accounts.

Effective risk management is crucial to safeguarding your capital. One strategy to prevent complete account depletion is to adjust your margin levels in response to losses at predefined intervals. For example, you could decrease your investment by 20% each time your account registers a 10% loss.

Month 1: $1000   -   Margin = ×1,2

Month 2: $850   -   Margin = ×1

Month 3: $700   -   Margin = ×0,6

Month 4: $600   -   Margin = ×0.4

Month 5: $500   -   Margin = ×0.2

This is just an example; it is up to you to define your rules and calculate where your loss would stop. Secondly, if you can't beat broad indexes, just buy them. Therefore, you could adapt this approach by buying more indexes the more you lose money.

Fourth part

PERSONAL FINANCE

Welcome to the realm of personal finance. In this chapter, we will delve into the essential topics of saving money and budgeting. As investors, managing our budget is crucial; it's our only way to prosper. Personal finance encompasses a wide array of aspects, including budgeting, saving, investing, debt management, retirement planning and more. It is surprising to observe the prevalent lack of financial management skills among individuals. Believe me or not, with a wise personal finance and basic understanding on ETFs, anyone can become millionaire in their lifetime.

Compensating vs growing

Experiencing a sense of logic is truly empowering. However, when it comes to money, many people mistakenly believe they possess logical thinking due to a lack of awareness. Despite my young age, I've observed numerous cases where individuals adopt a "compensation" mindset in managing their money and budget. This implies that if you give them

$1000, they will spend it within a few days, or, conversely, if they eliminate an expense, they will find a new one at the same cost. Living a life constantly compensating for earnings and expenses hinders wealth accumulation.

Compensating for both earnings and expenses gives a great feeling to the individual; he enjoys his logic: "This happened, so I can do that". Another way to see it is that it's a great excuse to justify expenses and another is to note that the individual doesn't even realize he could save that money to work on his freedom.

My only explanation for this common phenomenon is, indeed, the lack of awareness. I believe that if these people knew how rich they could get by managing their money, they would behave in a completely different way. As for you, dear reader, the simple fact that you are reading this shows that you are on the right path.

Compensating for every flow of money is detrimental. However, your profits in trading can be an exception to this, as the optimal time to withdraw funds from your investments is during the most profitable periods. If you are genuinely willing to spend, then you could indeed do it in your best months. By doing this, you can slightly decrease your invested amount when the market is at its peak and spend less when the market is low. Additionally, it is crucial to appreciate your successes and avoid being in a perpetual state of dissatisfaction, always chasing the next goal.

Assessing your current financial situation

It is crucial to assess your current financial situation. Evaluating your finances provides a snapshot of your income, expenses, assets, liabilities and overall financial health.

Contrary to what most people think, tracking our financial situation is not a daunting task. The simplest and most efficient way to track your money is by calculating your net worth every month. Your net worth is the difference between your assets and liabilities. List all your assets, including cash, savings, investments, property and vehicles. On the 1st of each month, check all your bank accounts and write down each amount in a document to calculate the sum. You should also identify your liabilities, such as credit card debt, student loans, mortgages and other outstanding loans. This practice helps you understand your financial standing. By creating this monthly habit, which takes only 5 minutes, you will be able to generate a graph of your net worth and calculate your average yearly performance.

Performance overview

Setting goals can be an effective way to efficiently accumulate wealth, as long as they do not overly increase your stress or disturb your well-being. Goals provide direction, motivation and a benchmark against which you can measure your progress.

The average yearly performance you can achieve will vary tremendously based on your competence in all that trading involves and your personality. While some may lose money, the best can achieve a performance of 30% or more. Nonetheless, the chart below will illustrate my estimation of the average performances you can expect by being serious and consistent. This chart is, of course, extremely speculative and generalized.

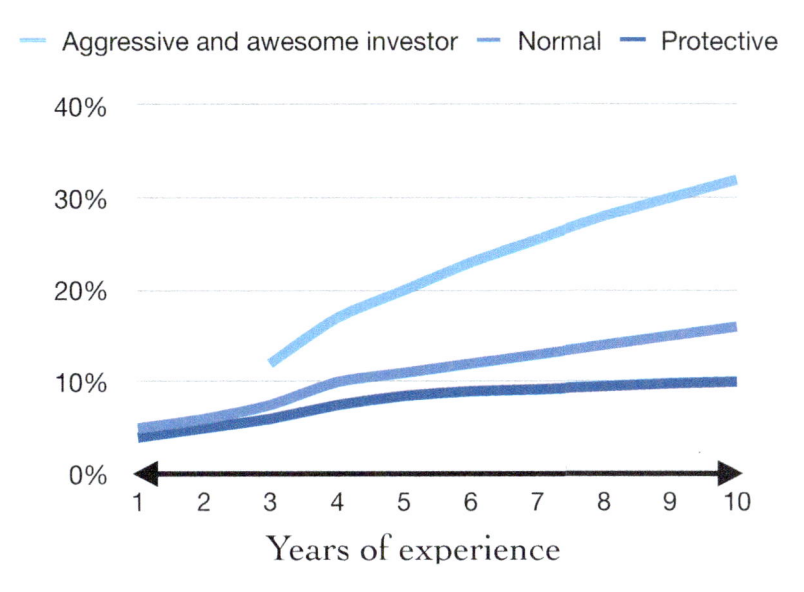

Aggressive and awesome investor — Normal — Protective

```
40%
30%
20%
10%
 0%
     1  2  3  4  5  6  7  8  9  10
            Years of experience
```

As you noticed, there is no aggressive estimation for less than 3 years of experience, as beginners should never start with it. Note that if I had to include this aggressive part, the average performance may be below zero for these first years.

You can also note a significant increase in performance after 3-4 years. I do indeed believe that this will be the time required for you to understand the market as it is. After 3 to 4 years, you will have a keen eye on the market and by this time, you will certainly have identified what you're good at and find the approach that resonates with you. Also, keep in mind that every year is different; therefore, compare your performance to the indexes themselves. If your performance is lower, then trade less and increase your investments in broad indexes. Finally, remember that there are inherent losses when starting, but they will be part of your experience.

Dependence:

At this level, most people will not be able to survive with their sole investment activities.

Financial freedom:

The orange level is the one that can be considered as the start of financial freedom as only 5% per year will probably be enough for you to survive.

Prosperity:

Millionaires are in green and represent about 1.1% of the world's populations. At this level you can easily quit your job.

World impact:

Billionaires start at the blue. This represents only about 2700 individuals in the world.

Richest persons on earth:

At this level you will be part of the 100 persons who posses half of the money on earth.

Projection of your net worth

10K	5%	10%	15%	20%	25%	30%	40%	50%
10 years	$16K	$26K	$41K	$62K	$93K	$138K	$289K	$577K
20 years	$27K	$67K	$164K	$383K	$867K	$2M	$8M	$33M
30 years	$43K	$175K	$662K	$2M	$8M	$26M	$242M	$2B
40 years	$70K	$453K	$3M	$15M	$75M	$361M	$7B	$111B
50 years	$115K	$1M	$11M	$91M	$701M	$5B	$202B	$6.376B

100K	5%	10%	15%	20%	25%	30%	40%	50%
10 years	$163K	$259K	$405K	$619K	$931K	$1M	$3M	$6M
20 years	$265K	$673K	$2M	$4M	$9M	$19M	$84M	$333M
30 years	$432K	$2M	$7M	$24M	$81M	$262M	$2B	$19B
40 years	$704K	$5M	$27M	$147M	$752M	$4B	$70B	$1.106B
50 years	$1M	$12M	$108M	$910M	$7B	$50B	$2.025B	$63.762B

With a performance of 26% per year, a net worth does times 10 every 10 years, meaning times 100 every 20 years. Think about it.

Below are other ways to achieve a tenfold performance.

3 trades of 116%.

5 trades of 59%.

15 trades of 17%.

30 trades of 8%.

80 trades of 3%.

232 trades of 1%.

Lastly, as the impact of compound interest is hard to measure for the human brain, it is worth computing the average income you predict to have throughout a given period. For instance, if you have $100K and earn 15% per year, you could focus on the average income instead of the current income. You would indeed earn $15,000 this year, but in fact, your average yearly income in the following 20 years will be around $66,000. Keeping your average income for the following years in mind, instead of your current income, will help you stay focused and motivated on your journey.

Expenses

When striving for greater wealth, it's illogical to invest significant efforts in increasing your earnings without also focusing on reducing your expenses. Saving money is undeniably part of an investor's responsibility, as the more you save, the more you can invest.

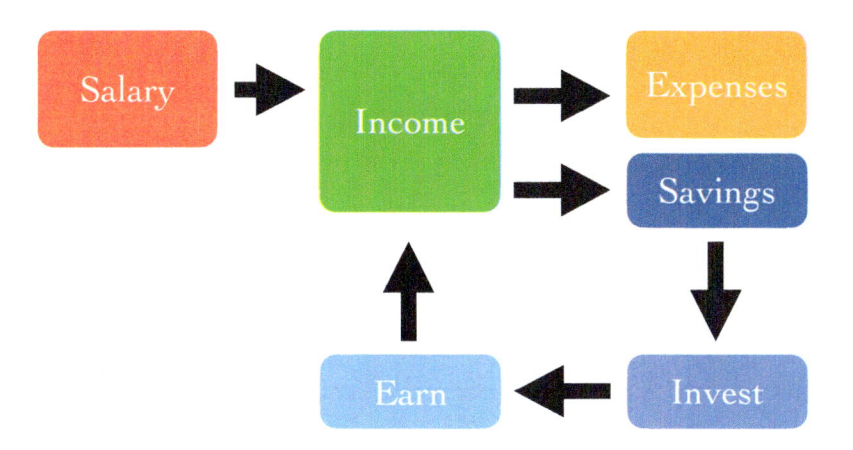

The importance of saving is determined by the size of your investments compared to your income.

At the core of your expenses is your perception of what your needs are. The concept of "needs" warrants clarification and it is undoubtedly a relative one. Our true needs are those of basic survival: a residence, clothes, food, water, etc. Nevertheless, in today's society, the consensus on needs has evolved considerably. We find ourselves needing clothing not only for essential purposes but also for work, social engagements, various sports and for crafting an image in the eyes of others. We feel the need for that glass of wine with friends. We want a nice car and the latest trendy mobile phone model. The desire to travel on vacations becomes a necessity in itself. Our list of "needs" has expanded to the point where it seems challenging to allocate a portion of our income, from whatever source, to savings, as I have emphasized earlier. There is no problem in spending, but there's a problem in spending if we are not financially free.

Hence, it is imperative to have a very clear view of your expenses. Can they be easily tightened and are you willing to make those adjustments?

Let's be practical. Approximately 1% of your purchases likely account for around 70% of your expenses. Therefore, it's crucial to focus on this 1%, which often includes your residence and your car.

For ambitious investors, choosing to buy a house to live in and owning a car are not the most favorable options for achieving significant growth. Opting for alternatives to car ownership and renting rather than purchasing your residence can have a substantial impact on your future wealth. Studies indicate that many millionaires, contrary to popular belief, tend to prefer second-hand cars. Cars lose 20% of their value as soon as they are bought for the first time and between 30% to 50% after being driven for just 2 years. While there's nothing inherently wrong with these choices, making such adjustments could save you thousands of dollars that can be invested for future growth.

Another significant area where you can easily reduce expenses is in your food budget. Opting to avoid fast food and restaurants can lead to substantial savings. When you prepare meals at home, the cost is often significantly lower than dining out. For instance, making your own sandwiches for lunch at work or purchasing potatoes at a grocery store instead of opting for French fries at a fast-food restaurant can effectively halve these expenses.

As extreme as it may sound, I personally don't make any purchase above 1% of my net worth when I don't see it as a genuine investment.

By sharing these ideas, people tend to see the dark side of it and forget that all the money they don't spend is well stacked in a safe spot. In other words, being frugal and avoiding unnecessary expenses is not a setback because you keep that money elsewhere.

Reaching consistency

Allow me to discuss a brief section on personal development. You might believe that reducing your expenses will demand a great deal of discipline. However, discipline is, in fact, a significant lie. It entails intrinsic resistance and is unlikely to yield significant results in your life.

The true game-changer is your identity. Your identity defines your choices; it tells your brain what is best. Therefore, if you identify yourself as someone in good health and shape, you will naturally not be attracted to sugar and you will engage in physical activity without mental effort. The same applies to your expenses. If you change your identity to someone who saves a lot of money for a better future, your actions will be oriented in that direction with no effort.

In short, there is no need for discipline when you do things naturally. The only way to do things naturally is to change your identity and values.

Think of it. What part of your life's results have truly been determined by discipline and what part came from your natural behaviors and values?

Simple budgeting

Finally, if you want to track your finances in more detail, create a list of all your earnings and expenses categorized. Here is an example:

Money In	$
Salary	2.300 US$
Additional income	300 US$
Yearly income	31.200 US$
Monthly income	2.600 US$
Daily income	87 US$

Money Out	$
Housing	1.300 US$
Shopping	450 US$
Electricity	35 US$
Transport	60 US$
Others	75 US$
Yearly expenses	23.040 US$
Monthly expenses	1.920 US$
Daily expenses	64 US$

Money Left Over	$
Yearly saved	8.160 US$
Monthly saved	680 US$
Daily saved	23 US$

- Transport 2%
- Electricity 1%
- Shopping 17%
- Housing 50%
- Others 3%
- Monthly saved 26%

"The average person can become a millionaire in their lifetime by increasing their revenue by 30% and investing that increase wisely."

Fifth part
TECHNICAL ANALYSIS

The technical analysis is essentially the study of historical prices to predict future trends. It's usually done with charts. As mentioned previously, TradingView is the best website to analyze charts.

This last chapter will cover advanced trading techniques meant to enhance your investments. You should indeed see trading as the optimization of your investments and not as an investment itself. The first step on your trading path must be ETFs and long-term investments. As you gain confidence and experience, you can gradually start the "real" trading, using technical analysis. I repeat, it should only be used to enhance your performance. Keep fundamental analysis as a priority and trade on top of that.

Before delving into this in-depth chapter, it's essential to understand that the price goes where it wants, or better said, it goes where it goes. There is no way to predict a price move with certainty; however, there are indications that tend to be true.

In short, there is no magic indicator, as the price moves somewhat randomly. On the other hand, it's challenging to make decisions without indicators and there's no doubt that they help understand the price's history more accurately.

Trends and ranges

The price can be in an uptrend, a downtrend or in a range.

An uptrend is typically characterized by higher highs and higher lows, while a downtrend is marked by lower highs and lower lows. As for a range, it means that the price moves sideways. The longer the range, the stronger the following uptrend or downtrend is supposed to be.

Dow's theory

Basic trading identifies reversals with changes occurring at peaks (highs) and valleys (lows). In Dow's theory, we usually define trends as follows:

Uptrend:

An uptrend is characterized by both higher highs and higher lows. In other words, the last peak and low need to be higher than the previous ones.

Downtrend:

A downtrend is characterized by both lower highs and lower lows.

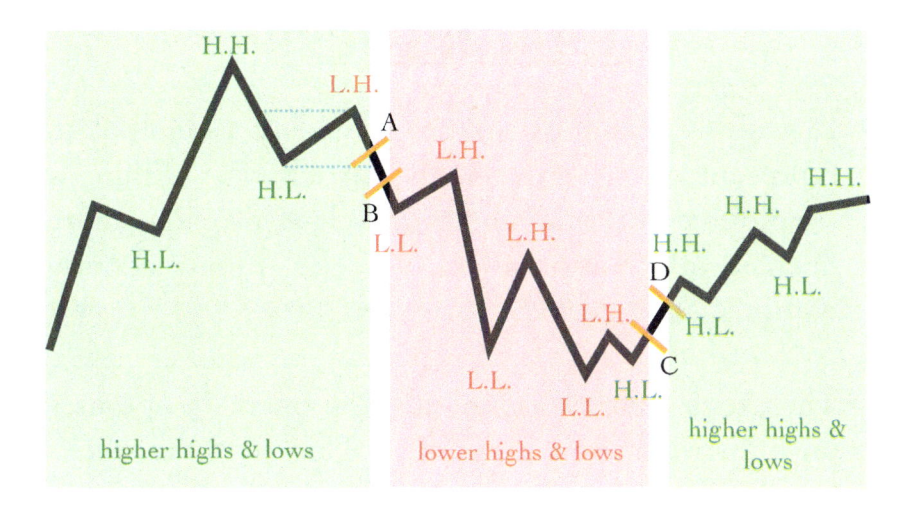

A. Confirmation of a lower high

B. Confirmation of a lower low

C. Confirmation of a higher low

D. Confirmation of a higher high

When it comes to actual trading, identifying reversals may not be as straightforward since fluctuations can occur in all timeframes. However, it is a very basic concept of trading to always keep in mind.

Candlesticks

In trading, candlesticks are a widely used tool to represent price movements on charts. Unlike a simple line chart, a candlestick chart provides more detailed information about a stock's trading activity within a given period.

The stock market is not always open; it operates during specific hours and days. This gives the stocks four key prices every day:

- the opening price (first price)

- the highest price

- the lowest price

- the closing price (last price)

We refer to these as OHLC prices.

Candlesticks represent these prices within a given period in a more visual way. Each candlestick is a shape that illustrates the opening, closing, high and low prices of a stock. The upper and lower lines of the candlestick are called shadows or wicks, while the main rectangular part is referred to as the body.

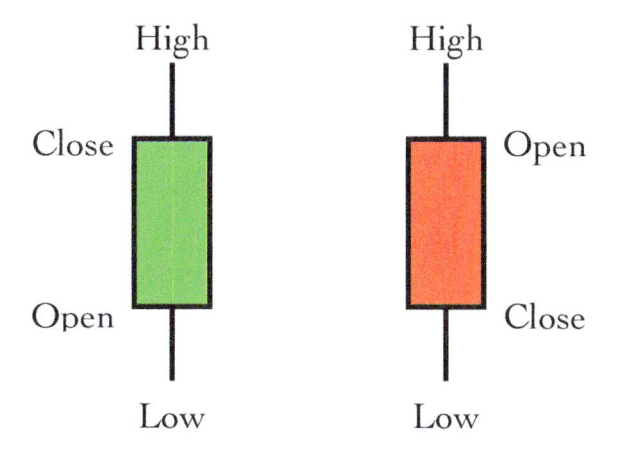

Candlesticks are typically colored green or red. A green candlestick indicates a price increase during the period, signifying that the closing price is higher than the opening price. Conversely, a red candlestick signifies a price decrease, indicating that the closing price is lower than the opening price.

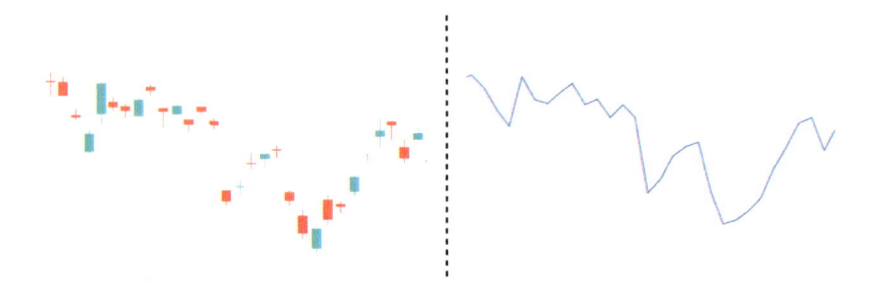

Utilizing candlesticks is more informative than relying on line charts as it offers four times more information about price movements. While we previously discussed candlesticks representing days, it's important to note that they can work with any timeframe. For instance, in a "daily" timeframe, one candle represents one day. In a "weekly" timeframe, one candle corresponds to one week and so on.

Interpretations

By studying the candlesticks, traders can determine market trends and identify potential buying or selling opportunities. Think of the candlestick as a visual representation of the war between buyers and sellers, akin to a battle for territory. Buyers aim to claim territory above, while sellers endeavor to push it down. Candlesticks reveal a summary of the dynamics of the battle within each specified period.

The doji

The doji holds significant importance in trading. Identified by two long shadows and a minimalistic body at the center, it forms a cross-like appearance. The doji signifies a moment of indecision in the market, where neither buyers nor sellers managed to assert control over the price.

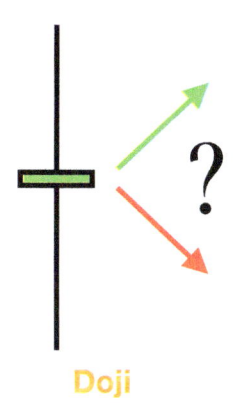

Doji

The two shadows indicate that both buyers and sellers had the potential to influence the market significantly, while the small centered body reflects the outcome of a standoff, where neither party emerged victorious.

While the presence of a doji in a trend does not necessarily indicate a reversal, it serves as a warning signal. A doji suggests a balance between buyers and sellers, signifying uncertainty about the trend's direction. When a doji appears, it indicates that the price has reached a point where both buyers and sellers are hesitant about the market's trajectory. This serves as a warning signal because, at this price level, opponents managed to block the price.

One of the most pertinent situations to use a doji is when you're already positioned in a trend. This could be an indication to close your position, as the doji represents uncertainty in the market.

The hammer and inverted hammer (and shooting star and hanging man when bearish)

The hammer and inverted hammer are candlesticks that indicate a potential reversal. They have a small body and a long shadow. The longer the shadow and the smaller the body, the stronger the signal. It is also more effective when the candlestick's direction is opposite to the trend (green if you want to buy, red if you want to sell).

Hammer   **Inverted hammer**

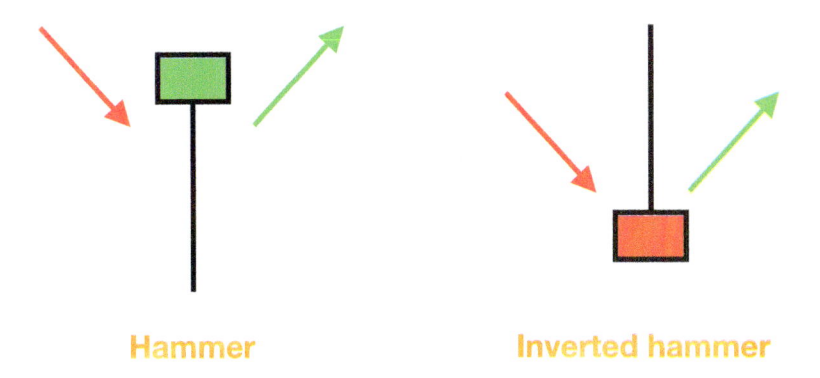

The hammer indicates that the price of the asset dropped significantly, but buyers ultimately emerged victorious.

On the other hand, the inverted hammer shows that the price hesitated to rise, that buyers are putting pressure on the price. While slightly weaker than the normal hammer, the inverted hammer can still be useful for traders. The bearish versions of these candlesticks are called the shooting star and hanging man.

No shadow at the close

A candlestick with a long body and no shadow on its closing side is often a signal of a reversal in the price trend.

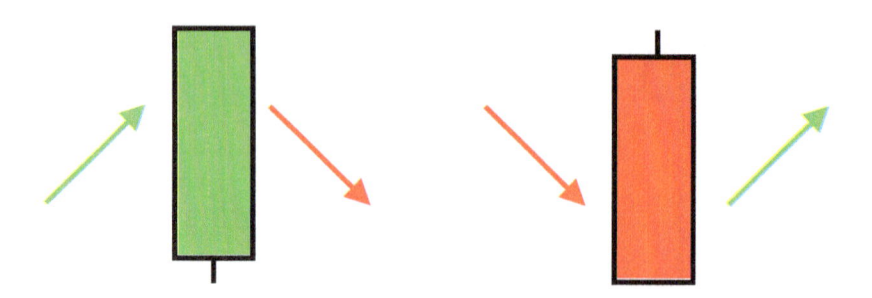

There are, of course, plenty of other candles, but I share the ones that are most crucial to know and useful in my trading. Experiment with different candlesticks and identify the ones that you prefer

Candlestick patterns

Candlestick patterns are a combination of candlesticks that can be considered as a signal of reversal or as a signal of continuation.

The piercing line and the dark cloud cover

Piercing line   **Dark cloud cover**

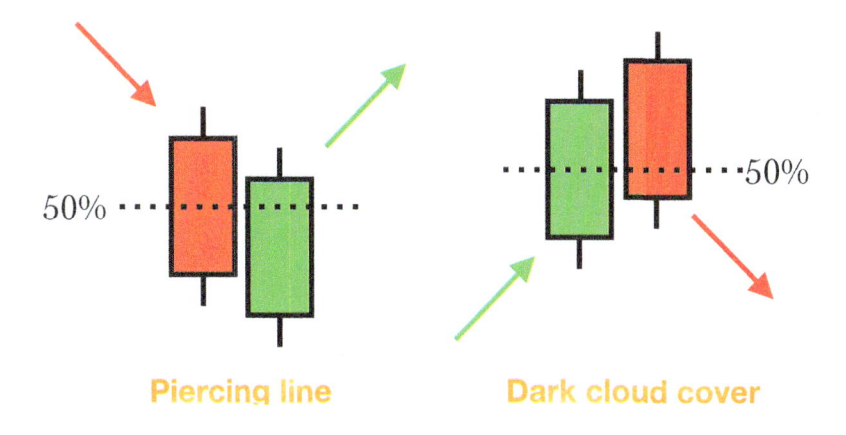

The piercing line is made up of two candles with large bodies, with the second one's body opening further but compensating more than 50% of the previous one; conversely for the dark cloud cover. They indicate that opponents start gaining strength.

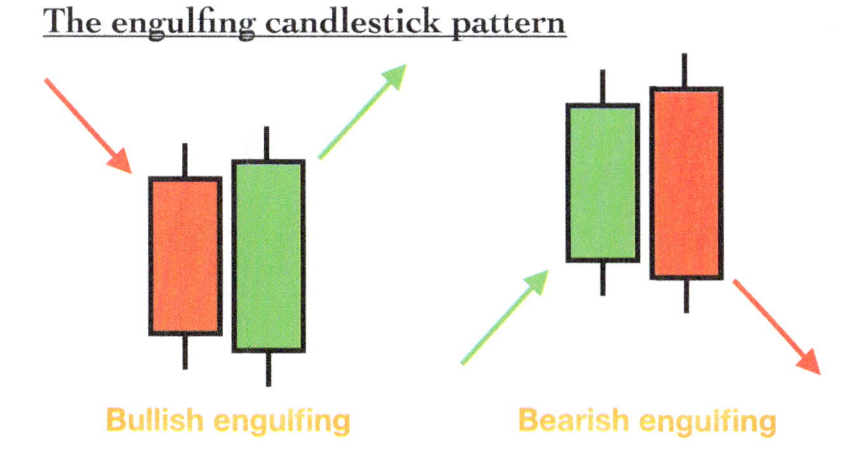

The engulfing candlestick pattern

Bullish engulfing   **Bearish engulfing**

While these two signals share similarities with the previously mentioned ones, the engulfing patterns retrace more than the previous candlestick rather than just more than 50%. These are stronger signals, indicating that the opponents of the trend have re-entered the market. The engulfing pattern tends to be highly effective.

Here, you can observe some of the patterns we've been discussing and witness their effectiveness:

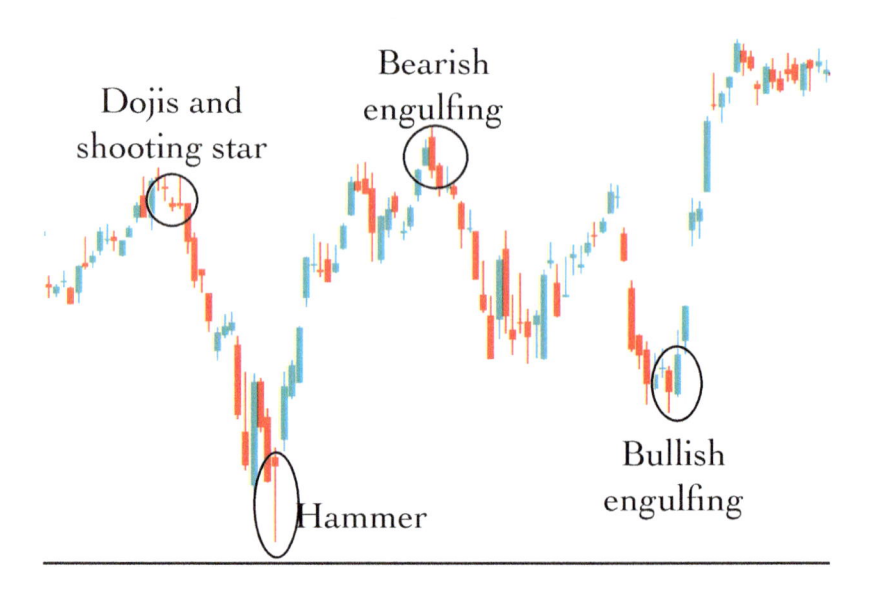

Heikin Ashi

Heikin Ashi candlesticks, among other variants of traditional candlesticks, serve as an effective tool in identifying trends and reducing noise in the market. In other words, they provide a nuanced depiction of price movements, making it useful to switch between normal candlesticks and Heikin Ashi ones during your trading.

Of course, no tool is flawless, but it serves as a good starting point.

Its calculation is simple, revolving around the concept of averages. The high and low of the Heikin

Ashi candlestick remain the same as the traditional one, but there are changes in the opening and closing prices:

Heikin Ashi O = (Previous O + Previous C) / 2

Heikin Ashi H = Maximum price during the period

Heikin Ashi L = Minimum price during the period

Heikin Ashi C = (O + H + L + C) / 4

These adjusted values craft candlesticks that emphasize trend clarity and mitigate market noise, presenting a potent solution to counteract false signals. They will be useful for what we will see at the end of this book.

However, Heikin Ashi candles come with two limitations. Firstly, they lack real-time pricing, as the closing value uses averaged values to create a smoothed representation, not reflecting the immediate current price of the asset. Secondly, they do not provide indications for candlestick patterns. Many of the candlestick patterns and signals we previously observed lose their direct applicability in Heikin Ashi charts.

Supports and resistances

A **support**, or support level, refers to a price level that an asset does not fall below for a period of time. This level is created by buyers entering the market whenever the asset dips to a lower price. The support line can be flat or slanted up or down with the overall price trend. Other technical indicators and charting techniques can be used to identify more advanced versions of support. On the other hand, **resistance** is the opposite – a price level that an asset does not surpass for a period of time.

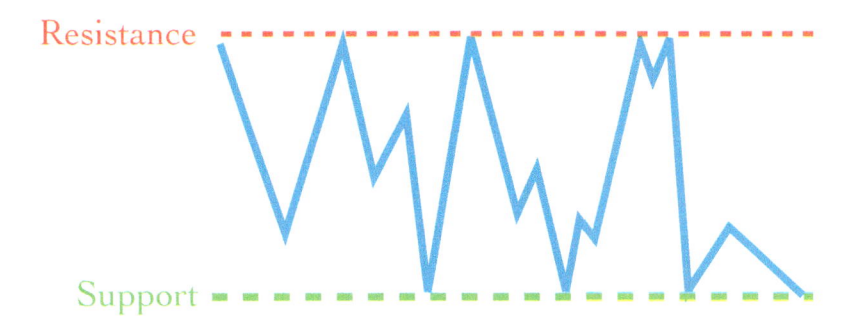

Once crossed, resistances become supports and supports become resistances.

Resistance becoming a support

Support becoming a resistance

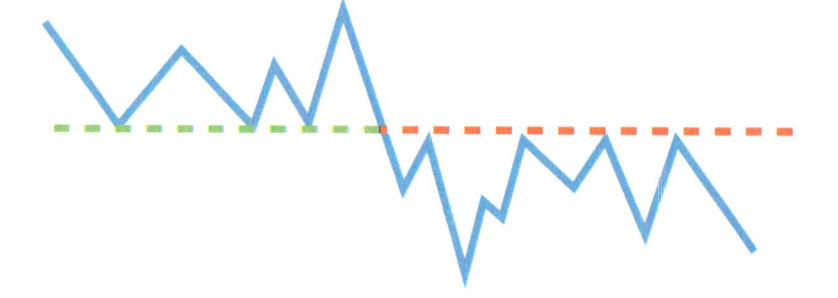

Support and resistance lines can also be diagonal.

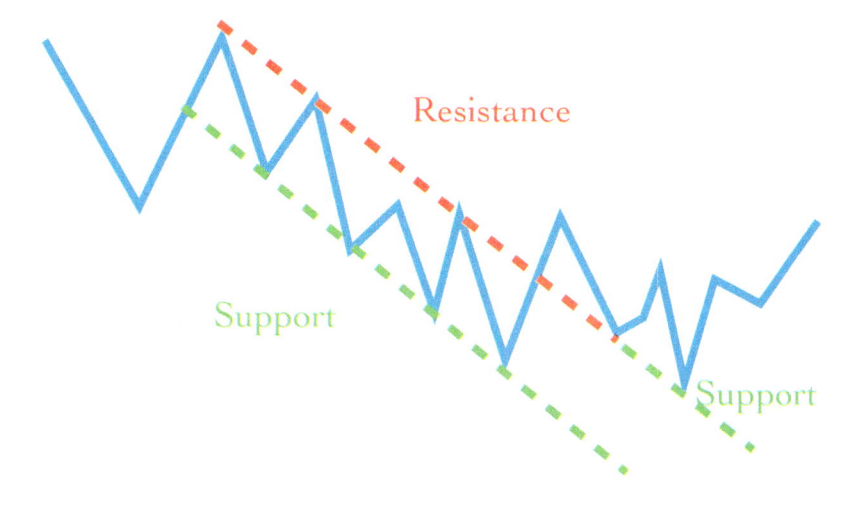

Horizontal lines offer the advantage of being directly associated with a fixed price (for example, the level of $22.10). However, it's essential to bear in mind that currency values fluctuate over time and what was valued at $22.10 five years ago may not hold the same worth today.

On the contrary, diagonal levels are temporary and will eventually go below zero or become too high. Nevertheless, they have the advantage of aligning with the price trend.

Note that a candlestick with a very long body can establish both strong support and resistance levels.

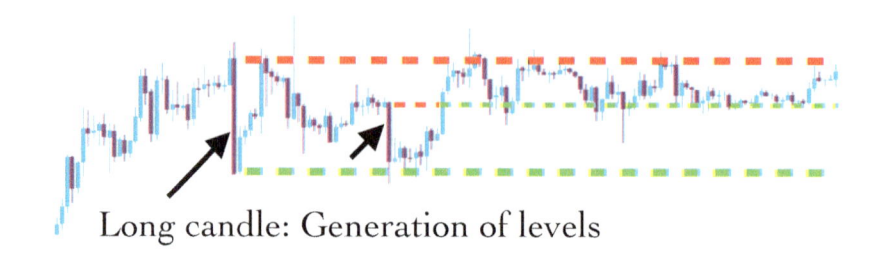

Long candle: Generation of levels

Breakouts

Breakouts, in trading, refer to a price surpassing a support or resistance level. Breaking a support level is considered a sell signal, while breaking a resistance level can indicate a buy signal.

A breakout is a significant signal in trading, signifying a notable shift in the supply and demand dynamics of a particular asset. When an asset's price has been moving within a relatively tight range for an extended period, it may reach a point where buyers or sellers become more dominant, causing the price to break out of that range. Moreover, breakouts often lead to substantial price movements, as ranges establish clear support and resistance levels, allowing traders time to prepare and place their orders above and below that range.

False breakouts

False breakouts occur when the price breaks through a support or resistance level but quickly retraces back into its previous trading range, resulting in losses for those who entered the trade based on the initial breakout.

As previously discussed, "whales", or large market players, often face liquidity issues, requiring a significant volume of orders going in the opposite direction to execute their trades successfully. In the absence of sufficient liquidity, their orders can cause rapid price movements before being fully filled. Some whales intentionally create breakouts to attract traders, subsequently placing their orders in their preferred direction. This manipulation serves as a means for them to obtain the necessary liquidity swiftly.

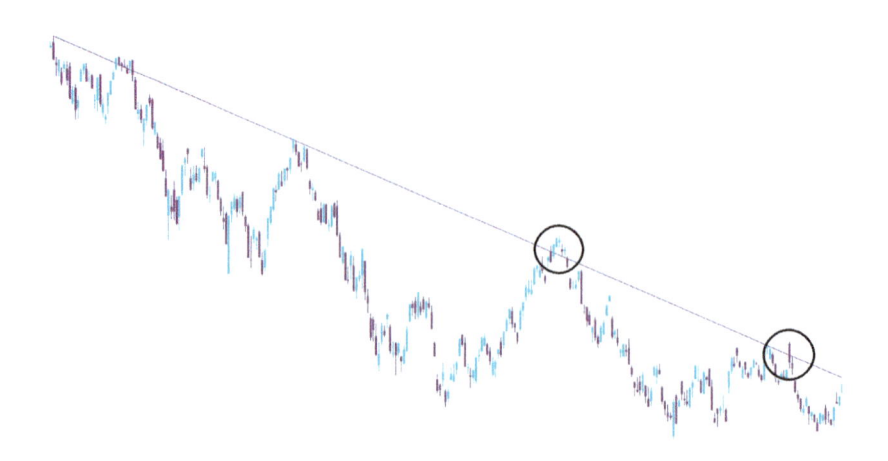

False breakouts can also result from temporary imbalances in supply and demand, often referred to as "noise" in the market. Another scenario is when the market tests a support or resistance level and once it fails to hold, traders quickly push the price back in the opposite direction.

While these instances may seem rare, they occur more often than one might think.

In short, confirming if a breakout has genuinely occurred is not straightforward, considering the presence of market noise and potential manipulation. False breakouts can be frustrating for traders, but there are effective ways to mitigate their impact. The standard approach is to wait for the candle to close outside the designated level. However, in today's market dynamics, it is advisable to exercise additional patience. Here are three approaches I use:

- Waiting for two, three, or even four closing prices outside the level.

- Waiting for two closes of the Heikin Ashi candlesticks outside the level.

- Waiting for a quick moving average to be outside (covered later in the book).

- Waiting for a pullback / throwback.

Pullbacks and throwbacks

Pullbacks and throwbacks, as discussed earlier, occur once a support is crossed, transforming it into a resistance. Throwbacks happen when the price revisits a former support and pullbacks occur when it retraces back to a previous resistance right after a breakout.

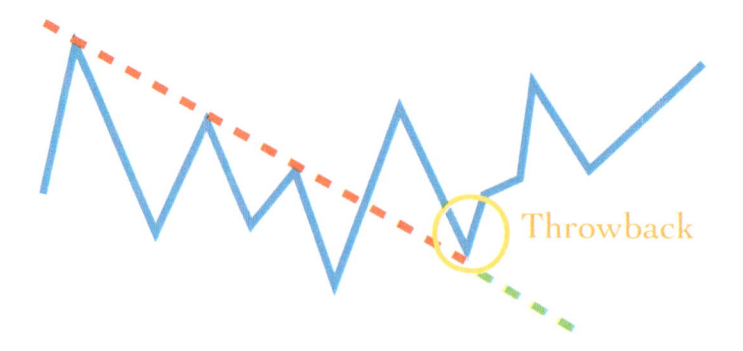

Opting to wait for a pullback or throwback rather than placing your order at the breakout point can provide a more favorable entry with a stop-loss positioned closely. Witnessing an effective pullback serves as a robust signal, enhancing the credibility of the breakout. However, it's important to note that pullbacks and throwbacks don't always occur. The decision lies with you: wait for confirmation through a pullback for a potentially better price or risk missing the trade if it doesn't materialize.

Gaps

Gaps in trading occur when there's a discontinuity or break in price between two consecutive trading sessions. This means that no trades happen within that price range during the gap. Think of it as a "no trading zone". Gaps can tell us a lot about what's happening in the market.

When you examine price charts, gaps manifest as empty spaces between two consecutive bars. These gaps can be classified as bullish, indicating a gap between the previous day's high and the current day's low, or bearish, with no trading occurring between the previous day's low and the current day's high. These gaps are not visible on a continuous line chart.

The common belief is that the price always returns to the level of the gap, we then say that the gap is "filled" or "partially filled". However, this is not always the case and the likelihood of gap filling depends on the type of gap. Gaps can indicate the strength of an existing trend, signal the end of a strong trend, or result from a momentary irregularity caused by significant news. Apart from that, gaps offer reliable support and resistance levels, simplifying the identification of optimal buying or selling points. In fact, some traders build their entire trading strategy around gap analysis.

Understanding the various types of gaps offers a significant advantage for stock market investors. Gaps represent short-lived market imbalances, typically arising from a mismatch between supply and demand. The crucial question is whether a gap is justified by a strong and lasting trend, be it an existing one or a new development. If not, the gap is often a temporary hiccup that doesn't significantly impact future prices. TradingView provides a useful indicator called "gaps" to identify and assess whether gaps have been filled or not.

TradingView provides a useful indicator called "gaps" to identify and assess whether gaps have been filled or not.

Common gap

These gaps are frequently observed in markets characterized by narrow price fluctuations. They typically occur in response to sudden news or during periods of low trading activity. Common gaps can take on a bullish or bearish nature and tend to be filled, boasting an approximately 90% fill rate within the first week in a daily timeframe. The trading volumes associated with common gaps are generally not significantly higher than the average volumes of exchanges of the past days, returning to normal levels swiftly. Unlike other gaps, common gaps typically do not evolve into lasting support or resistance levels.

Breakaway gap

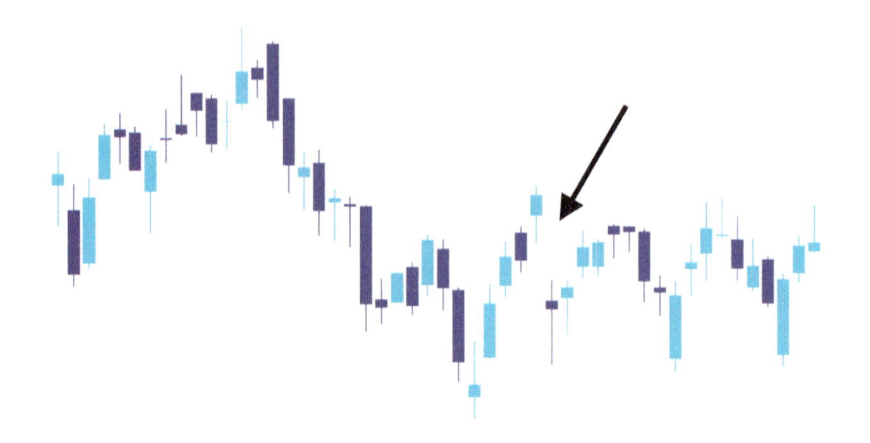

Breakaway gaps signal a strong upcoming trend. They occur in breakouts of supports, resistances, or chart patterns. You could call it a "breakout gap". These gaps validate the direction of the new trend and strengthen the reliability of chart patterns or support/resistance zones, particularly during trend reversals. These gaps are frequently accompanied by elevated trading volumes, typically reaching around twice the average daily volume, with a more pronounced increase for bearish gaps. These increased volumes often persist in the days following the gap, gradually decreasing.

Breakaway gap

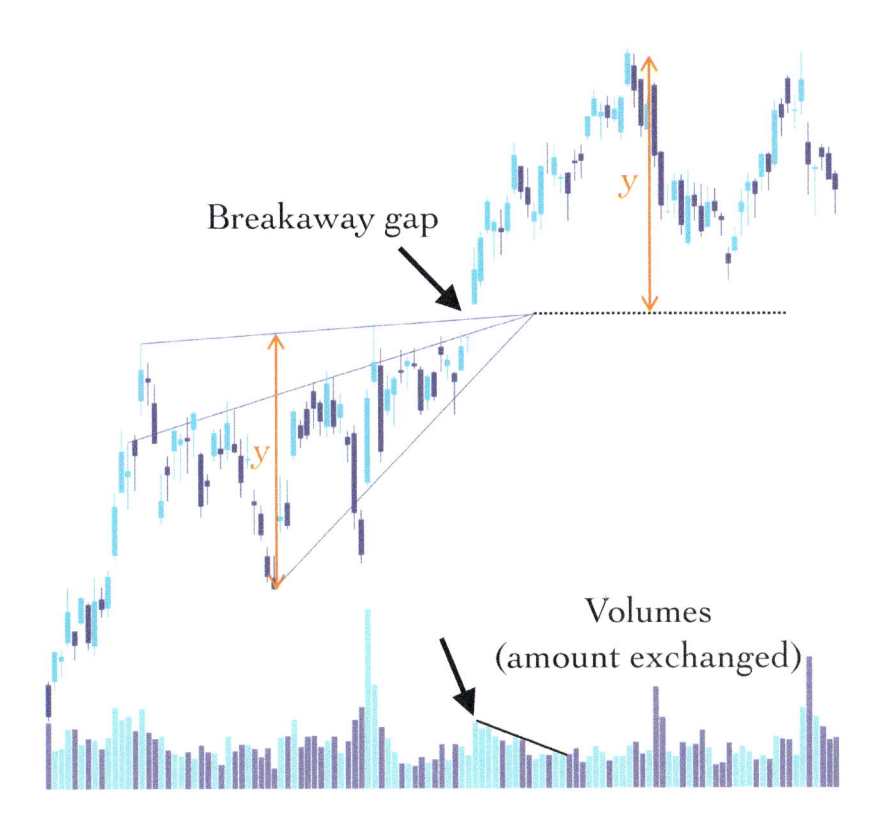

y

y

Volumes
(amount exchanged)

Be cautious of wide gaps that lack backing volumes because the gap arises from an imbalance between buying and selling volumes. In theory, the larger the gap's trading volume, the less likely it is to be filled. Such gaps are not typically meant to be filled immediately; sometimes, they are partially filled after a few days. In such instances, they evolve into robust support or resistance zones that can endure for an extended period. A complete fill of a breakaway gap within the first week is a rare occurrence (less than 5%and even rarer for bullish gaps). It would be a sign of weakness in the expected trend.

Runaway gap or Measuring gap

Runaway gaps manifest within a robust ongoing trend and validate its strength. They typically occur in the direction of the initial trend and often emerge around the halfway point of the trend, enabling traders to estimate a target price. Due to this characteristic, they are also referred to as measuring gaps. An initial target can be calculated by measuring the distance from the start of the trend to the runaway gap.

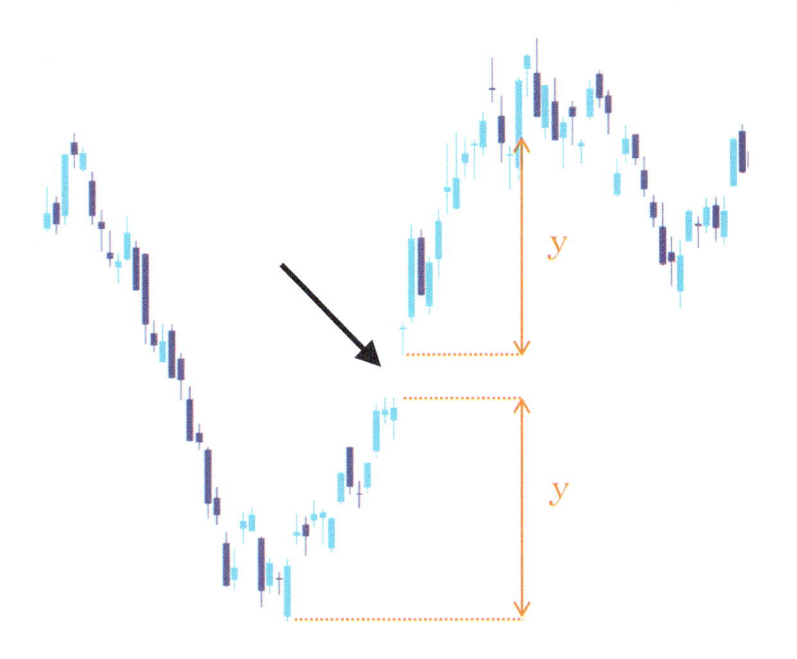

To be precise, runaway gaps typically amplify the previous trend by a factor of 2 to 2.2.

Multiple consecutive runaway gaps may occur. After three consecutive gaps in the same trend, the trend might pause or reverse. While runaway gaps are often tested, they usually aren't filled immediately, establishing themselves as support or resistance zones. In 90% of cases, they remain unfilled after a week. They not only confirm the ongoing trend but also provide a relatively precise target, encouraging low-risk positions in the direction of the initial trend.

Exhaustion gap

Speaking of multiple runaway gaps, exhaustion gaps occur at the end of a strong market move, sometimes made by these runaway gaps. The gap should align with the original trend's direction. These gaps are quickly filled, signaling a trend reversal. In 60% of cases for bullish gaps and 70% for bearish gaps, exhaustion gaps are filled within the first week. They often come with substantial trading volumes, approximately three times the average daily volumes, taking about a week to return to normal levels. These gaps serve as a grand finale for a trend that has run its course.

Island reversal

The island reversal is a unique gap formation that consists of two gaps, one bullish and one bearish (or vice versa), isolating a sequence of price movements from the rest of the price chart. It is a powerful signal of a major trend reversal, usually occurring at an extreme market level. Graphically, it creates a series of bar charts completely detached from the rest of the price chart, much like an island in the middle of the ocean.

Here's a quick summary of the main gaps we discussed.

Type of gap	Sign	Support	Filled*
Common	Small reversal	Weak	90% in a week
Breakaways	Strong move	Strong	5% in a week
Runaway	Strong move (double trend)	Weak	10% in a week
Exhaustion	Reversal	Moderated	65% in a week
Island reversal	Strong Reversal	Moderated	About 5% in a week

*daily timeframe

Manipulation

Manipulation in the market is orchestrated by very wealthy individuals and institutions, the easiest assets being the smaller ones - with low volumes. The most common types of manipulation can be identified with false breakouts or successive strong moves in the same direction at the opening.

False breakouts are often difficult to anticipate. Once they happen however, it probably means that a big whale is betting on the opposite direction.

The second type of manipulation occurs when the price makes a significant move at the opening but retraces back during the day. If this pattern appears successively every day, it is a sign that the price is being manipulated. The whales place huge orders to create a moment of greed, in the opposite direction in which they wish to bet. Once it's done, they smoothly revert their position to avoid detection. The manipulation can last 2 to 5 days, usually 3 and decreases every day. The reason they do it at the opening is mainly because they can take advantage of the premarket, which has about 10 times less volume.

Manipulation at the opening - three days before earnings day

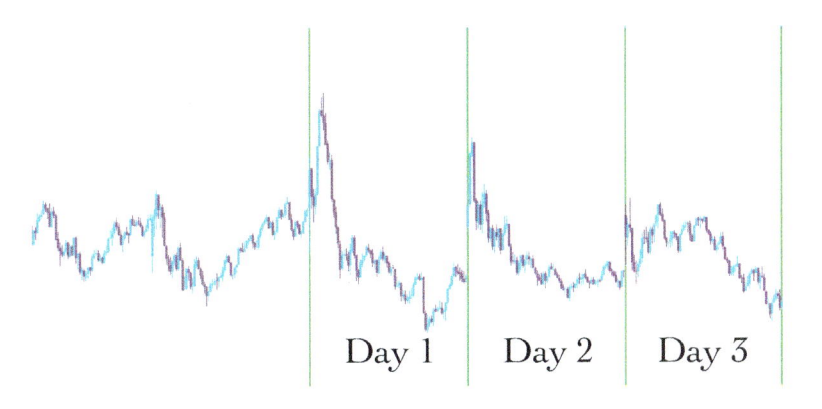

TSLA - 5 minutes - Jan 2023

In this example, the price dropped by -13% the very next day. It does seem that the manipulator had information on the earnings before they were released. Such practices, manipulating the price and having early information about earnings, are, of course, illegal, but they still happen a lot.

Momentum indicators

Momentum indicators are technical analysis tools used to determine the strength or weakness of an asset's price.

Period

Before delving into specific indicators, it's crucial to grasp the concept of the "period" associated with them. The period, also referred to as the indicator's length, is a crucial parameter determining the number of price data points considered in the calculation for each time period, whether it's daily, weekly, or per minute.

In other terms, an indicator provides a value related to each candlestick. The calculation of the indicator value for each candlestick typically involves the previous L prices, where L represents the length of the indicator. The length of an indicator is a key factor that influences its accuracy and sensitivity to market fluctuations.

For instance, a short-term indicator with a length of 10 periods considers the previous 10 candlesticks, while a longer-term indicator with a length of 50 periods uses the previous 50 candlesticks. Short-term indicators tend to react more quickly to price changes, whereas long-term indicators are more stable and less prone to noise. The length can be customized to fit a trader's specific trading strategy and timeframe.

If the length is too short, the indicator may generate too many signals, leading to false signals and resulting in losses. If the length is too long, the indicator may lag behind the price action, resulting in missed trading opportunities.

In general, shorter lengths are suitable for day traders or scalpers seeking quick profits and willing to take on higher risk. Longer lengths are more suitable for swing traders looking for more significant indications. It is recommended for beginners to start using the default values on their indicators.

The Relative strength index

The Relative Strength Index (RSI), the most popular momentum indicator, is displayed as an oscillator (a line graph that moves between two extremes) which has a reading from 0 to 100.

The calculation involves a somewhat complex formula, with the fundamental idea being to illustrate the average gains and losses over a specific period. By default, the RSI is set to a length of 14 periods, implying that each calculation incorporates the 14 preceding prices. However, some traders prefer a length of 21 periods for a smoother indicator reading.

There are 3 levels that are automatically displayed in the RSI: 30, 50 and 70.

One of the most effective ways to trade with the RSI is to analyze the area in which it is. The RSI has four areas defined by its three levels.

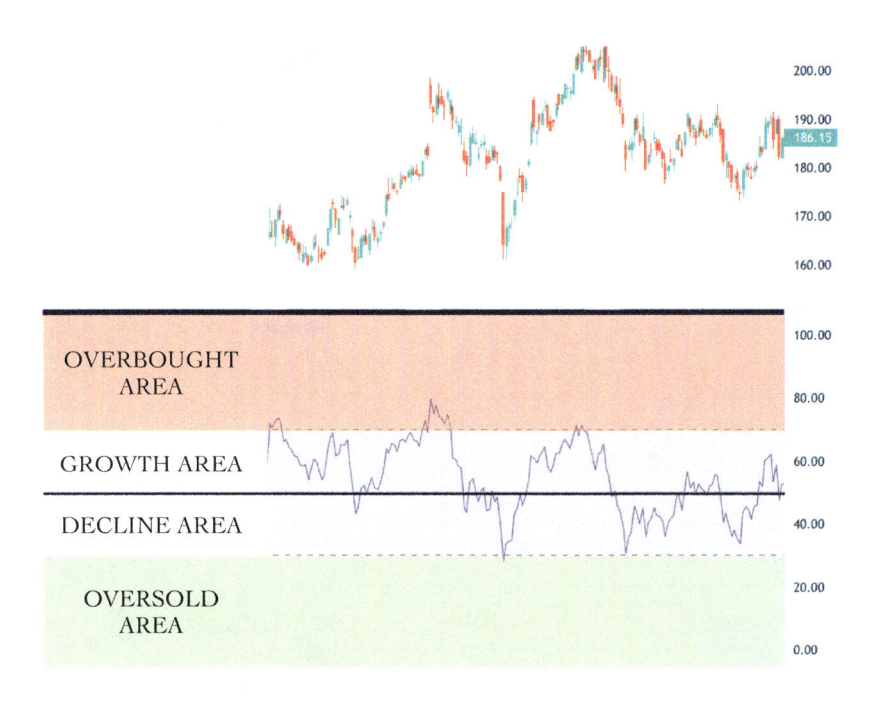

Overbought [70,100]: sell signal

Growth area [50,70]: buy signal

Decline area [30,50]: sell signal

Oversold [0,30]: buy signal

Upon closer examination of the chart, a notable price support emerges around the $160 level, coinciding with the RSI entering the oversold area. This convergence serves as a strong buy signal. Nevertheless, for long-term considerations, it is generally safer to initiate a purchase when the RSI enters the growth area rather than the oversold one.

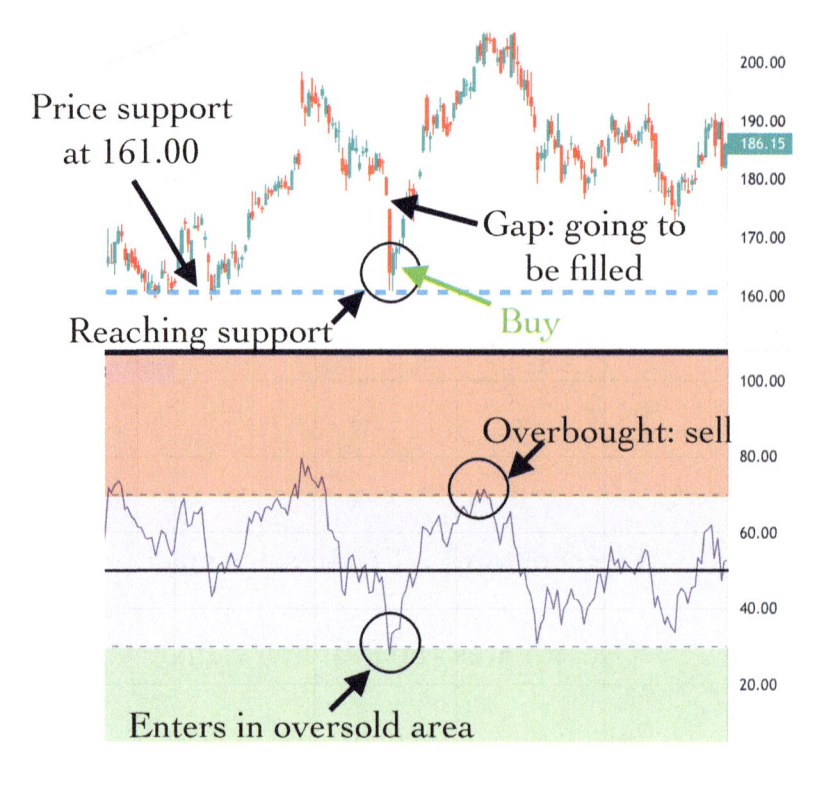

Price support at 161.00

Gap: going to be filled

Reaching support

Buy

Overbought: sell

Enters in oversold area

The moment to sell is also evident here. Following the entry into the trade, two runaway gaps occurred. Thus, we just need to wait for the trend to double.

Furthermore, the RSI simultaneously reaches the overbought area.

The RSI also has supports and resistances. The probabilities for the RSI to bounce back are high at these three levels: 30, 50 and 70. Each asset will have its own unique levels. In this example, you can observe that the RSI also reacts at the 43 and 65 levels, for instance.

Choppiness index

The choppiness index (CHOP) is an indicator that measures the potential energy of an asset's price movement. Unlike the RSI, it does not indicate the direction of the expected movement but only its strength. This makes it useful for determining whether a significant move is imminent or if the price is exhausted. The indicator's value also ranges from 0 to 100. Simply put, the choppiness index can be thought of as a measure of energy in the market and the more the price consolidates, the more energy it has. It helps to identify future periods of high and low volatility.

There are two important levels to consider when analyzing the choppiness index:

- When the CHOP is above 61, it indicates that the price is highly charged and there is a high probability of a significant price move, either up or down.

- When the CHOP is below 38, it suggests that the price is exhausted and likely to consolidate, with less chance of a major move in either direction.

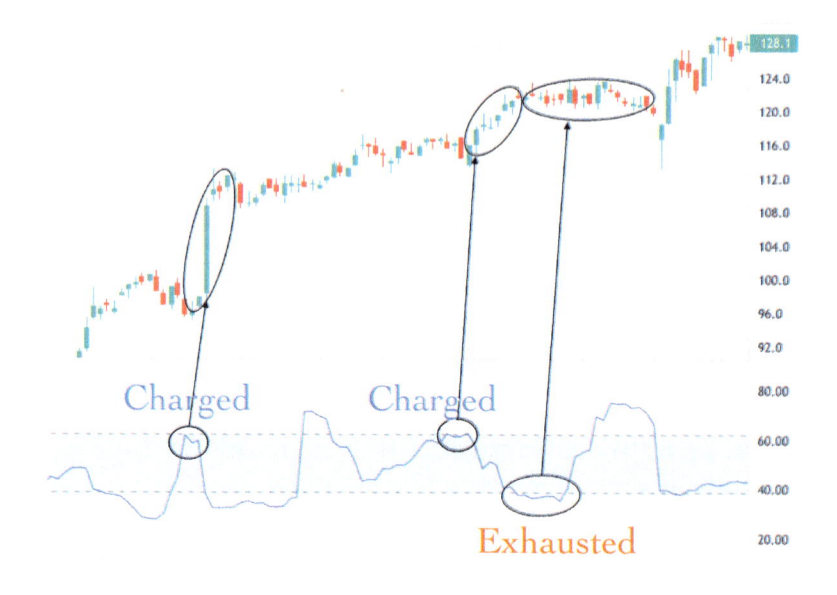

I like to compare the Choppiness Index to the weather. When there's a storm, the clouds release their water, so the probability that the weather will improve is high. Similarly, when the sky is clear blue, the probability that the weather will get worse is high. This indicator tells you about the two extremes of "it goes too fast" and "it goes too slow". Regarding the situation when the choppiness index is in the medium range, it suggests that there will be minimal alterations in the current trend.

Understanding how to use this indicator can be a little tricky at the beginning, as it doesn't predict a direction for the price. However, with practice, you will become comfortable using it and appreciate its usefulness.

RSI vs CHOP

After spending countless hours analyzing charts and programming indicators, I stumbled upon an interesting relationship between price movements and the differences between the RSI and CHOP indicators.

In particular, I noticed that when the RSI is above the CHOP, an uptrend is highly probable, while an RSI below the CHOP indicates a downtrend.

At first, this correlation seemed strange to me, but after extensive testing and analysis, I discovered that this relationship can provide valuable signals for traders. For instance, take a look at the weekly chart of Micron Technology, Inc (MU), where green candles represent an RSI(9) above CHOP(9)and red candles represent the opposite.

As you can see, this technique can yield good results; however, its effectiveness will vary for each asset. I recommend using a length of 9, although 11 and 13 can also work well. Although it should not be used alone, it may add a piece to your trading strategy. Keep in mind that nothing is perfect. If you don't have experience with coding (which is normal), here is the program for the indicator. You'll have to paste it into the "pine editor" section from TradingView to display it.

```
//@version=5
indicator("RSI-CHOP", overlay=false, timeframe="")
length = input.int(9, "Chop Length", minval=1)
ci = 100 * math.log10(math.sum(ta.atr(1), length) / (ta.highest(length) - ta.lowest(length))) / math.log10(length)
rsi=ta.rsi(close, length)
plotchop= plot(ci, "CHOP", color=color.new(#000000, 10), linewidth=1)
plotrsi=plot(rsi, "RSI", color=color.new(#000000, 10), linewidth=1)
fill(plotchop,plotrsi, color= rsi < ci ? color.new(#5f49d8, 25) : rsi > ci ? color.new(#90e1f0, 0) : #251515 )
barcolor = input(true, "Barcolor")
change = rsi > ci ? #00ccff : rsi < ci ? #8916e7 : #000000
barcolor(barcolor ? change : na)
```

Moving averages

Moving averages are very unique; unlike the oscillators we've seen before (separate from the price chart), moving averages overlay the price chart. They help smoothen the evolution of the price (eliminate volatility in our analysis) and provide a wide spectrum of strategies.

They simply represent the average of previous prices.

Considering Pn as the price of the current candlestick, n as the candlestick and L as the length of the moving average:

$$MA(P_n) = \frac{P_{n-0} + P_{n-1} + P_{n-2} + \ldots + P_{n-L}}{L}$$

In summary, we sum the L previous prices and then divide by L.

Here's an example:

	Length	Period 1	Period 2	Period 3	Period 4	Period 5	Period 6
Price		10	12	14	12	14	20
MA	2 periods	-	11	13	13	13	17
	4 periods	-	-	-	12	13	15

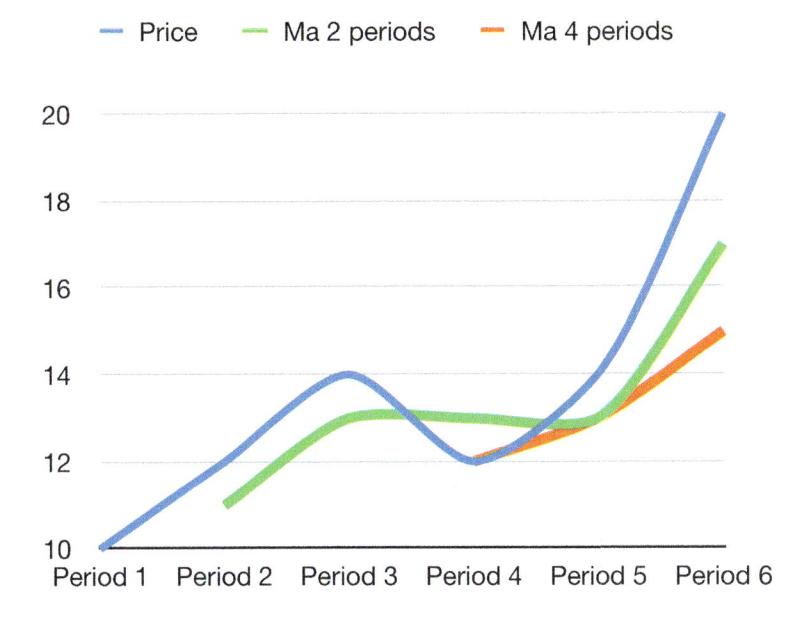

For instance, in the period 6:

MA 2 periods = (14+20) / 2

MA 4 periods = (14+12+14+20) / 4

This is how it really looks like when we add more price data:

MA 20 ━━
MA 50 ━━

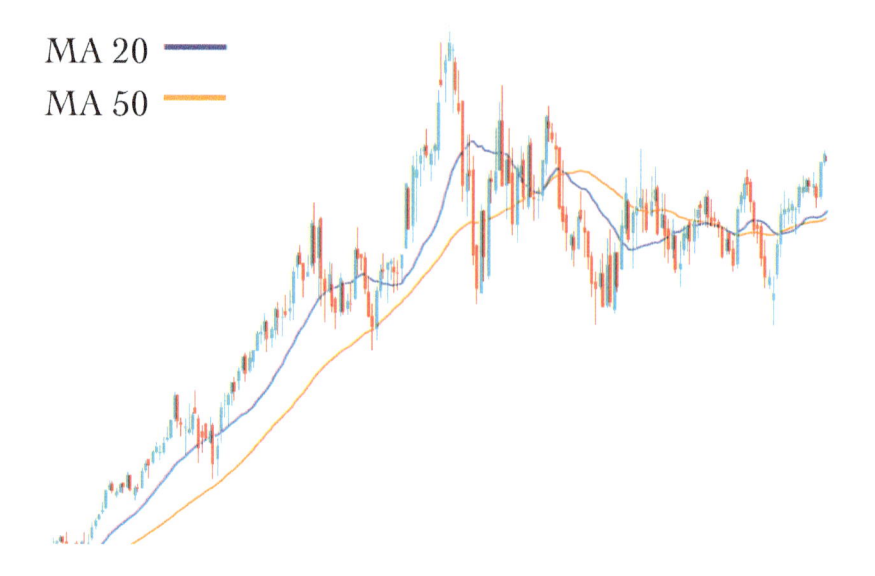

As you may have noticed, the length of a moving average plays a significant role in its responsiveness to price movements. Shorter lengths result in faster-moving averages, while longer lengths provide a more smoothed-out view of price action.

Now, let's dive into the trading part. There are three primary ways to use moving averages in trading:

The first one and one of the best, is to simply follow them:

1. Moving average(s) in an uptrend: buying

2. Moving average(s) in a downtrend: selling

The second way is to trade according to crosses. There are 4 options:

1. Price crossing above a MA: buying

2. Price crossing below a MA: selling

3. Fast MA (small length) crossing above a slow MA: buying

4. Fast MA crossing below a slow MA: selling

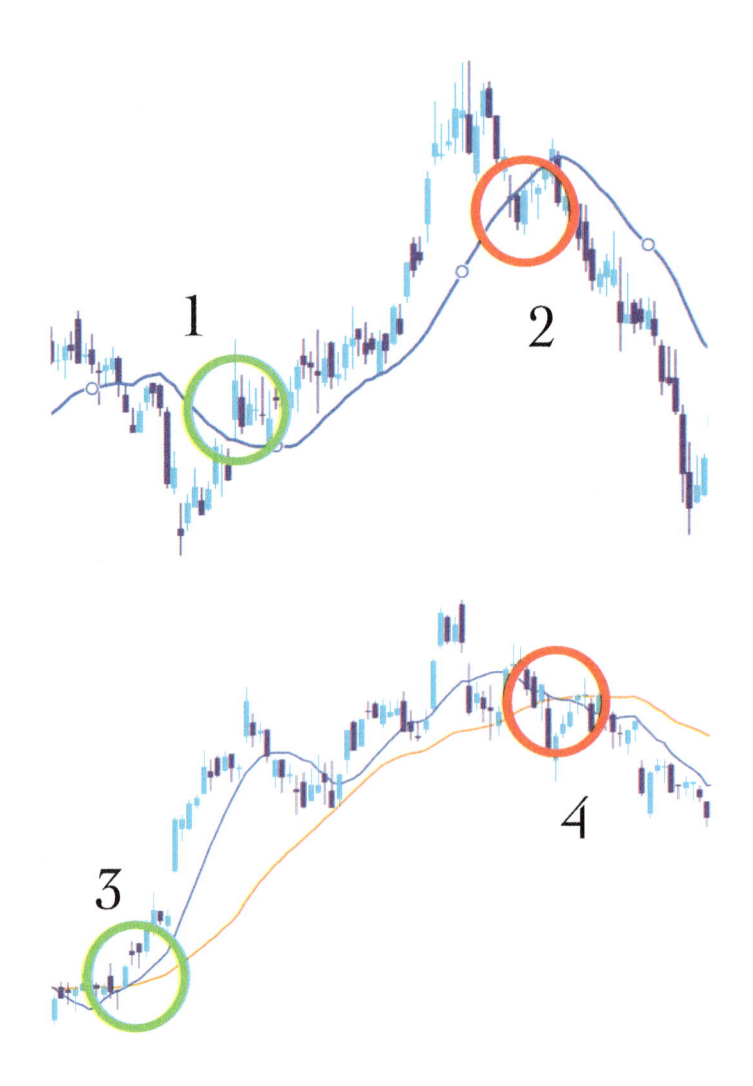

These events indicate that a new trend might be emerging.

196

The third way is to use them to analyze support and resistance levels. In this case, a high length is recommended.

1. Price reaching the MA from above: buying

2. Price reaching the MA from below: selling

The reason why prices often bounce on moving averages is that traders believe prices should follow a particular trend. For example, when a trader expects an uptrend, it means to them that the price should be above the moving average (because the MA is always late). As a result, when the price touches it, they believe the price will not go below it as the trend must be upwards and conversely for downtrends. These traders a so generating a lot of demand on those levels. Making the price bounce on the line.

Periods for moving avengers

The most commonly recommended periods for moving averages are 20, 50, 100, 200, or even 1000; with the 200 being an excellent one. These lengths are widely followed and used.

However, an underrated way of selecting lengths is by using time units (weeks, months, quarters, years, etc.). In this case, if you are in a daily timeframe, you will have to set a length of 252 if you want a yearly moving average since there is an average of 252 trading days per year in the stock market. For a monthly unit, you will need to set it at 21 periods (252/12=21) and 5 periods for a weekly moving average.

Quarterly MA — Yearly MA — 5 years MA —

This is my favorite way to use moving averages, as you can see, it gives very good signals and levels.

Other types of moving averages

The moving average we just saw is called a simple moving average (SMA). There are several other types of moving averages that exist, they can be an alternative to gain insights into market trends. Let's delve into a couple of them:

Exponential Moving Average (EMA):

The EMA, unlike the SMA, gives more weight to recent price data. In low timeframes, it is particularly effective with lengths of 40 and 80 periods. The exponential nature of this moving average allows it to react more quickly to price changes, making it useful when looking for more responsiveness in our analysis.

EMA 40, 80 & 100 in a 15 minutes chart

Least square

The least square moving average (LSMA), also called endpoint or linear regression moving average, stands out for its extreme speed as it places a weighted emphasis on recent price data. Therefore, it does not provide levels of support and resistance, but it does offer a good view of the trends.

Moving percentile

We mentioned averages from the beginning of this chapter; however, medians and quartiles also exist. Medians and quartiles are, in fact, what's called percentiles. In short, a percentile is the value at which x% of the data is below. Moving percentiles are not common, I might be their author, as I have never encountered them elsewhere.

Moving percentiles 0, 50 and 100 - 100 periods

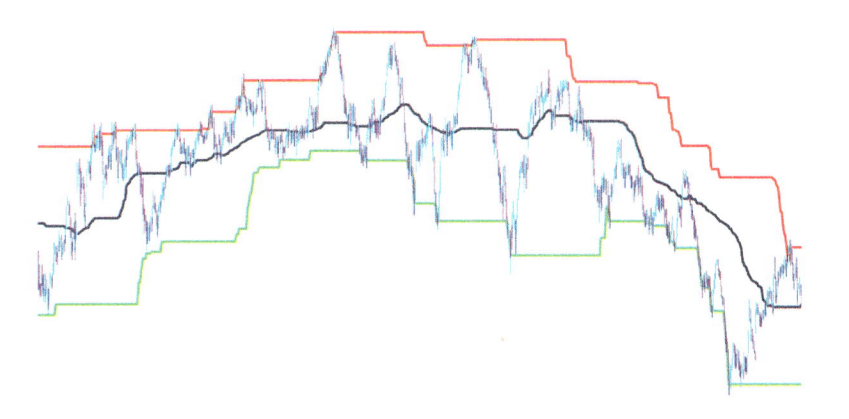

WTRG - Daily - 2021 to 2023

The green line represents the level at which 0% of the prices have been below for the past 100 periods; conversely, for the top. As for the black middle line, it represents the value at which 50% of the values in the last 100 periods are below.

Percentiles are very powerful when the price is in a large range, but they can also be utilized to track the trend.

Moving percentiles 25, 50 and 75 - 20 periods

Ichimoku cloud

The Ichimoku cloud is a famous indicator known for its impressive appearance. However, it is often misunderstood. The indicator is composed of 5 lines:

- Tenkan-sen (Conversion Line): This is the faster-moving line and is calculated by averaging the highest high and lowest low over a specific period (usually 9 periods). It provides short-term trend information.

- Kijun-sen (Base Line): This line is slower and is calculated like the Tenkan-sen but has a longer period (usually 26 periods). It provides medium-term trend information.

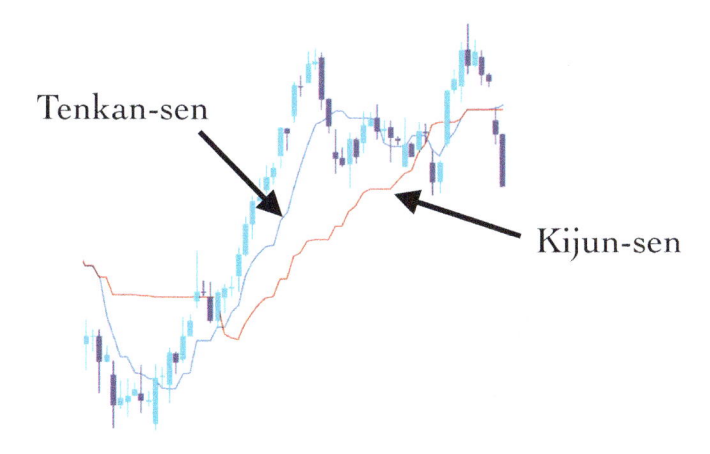

- <u>Senkou Span A</u> (Leading Span A): This line represents the average of the Tenkan-sen and Kijun-sen plotted 26 periods ahead. It forms the upper boundary of the cloud in uptrends.

- <u>Senkou Span B</u> (Leading Span B): It is calculated by averaging the highest high and lowest low over a longer period (usually 52 periods) and plotted 26 periods ahead. It forms the lower boundary of the cloud in uptrends.

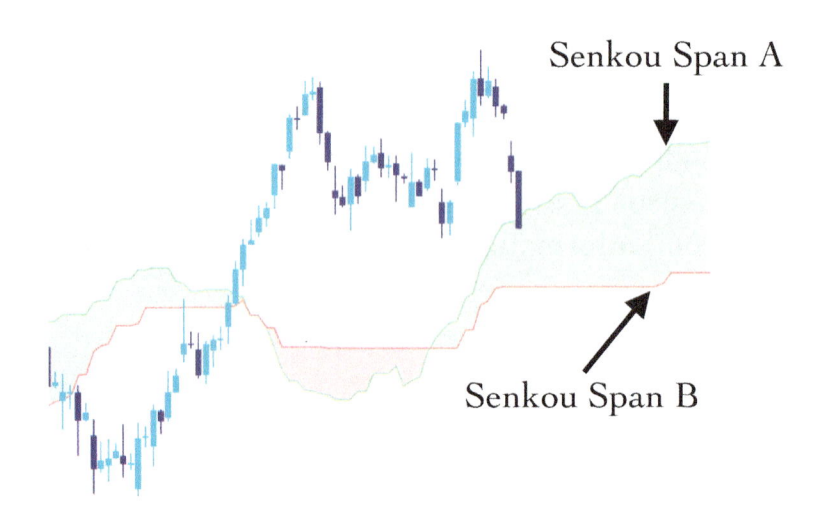

- <u>Chikou Span</u> (Lagging Span): This line simply represents the closing price, plotted 26 periods behind. It helps identify potential support or resistance levels. However, it is less useful than the other components of the Ichimoku cloud.

The area between Senkou Span A and the B is called the Kumo (Cloud). The cloud's color (green or red) depends on whether the Senkou Span A is above or below the Senkou Span B.

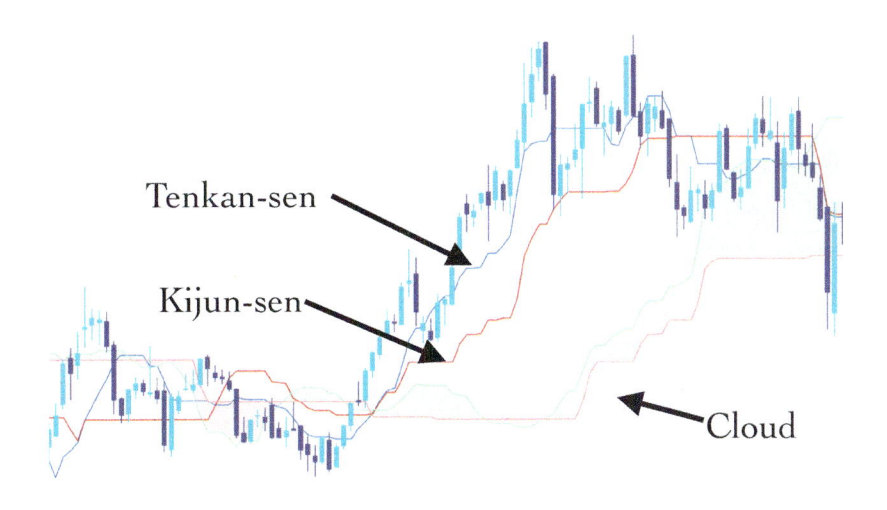

It's very important to note that the cloud has lag; it is plotted 26 periods ahead. The reason for this is to provide traders with a visual representation of future support and resistance levels. However, my personal recommendation is to get rid of this lag as it is more disturbing than useful. By doing so, both the Tenkan-sen and the Kijun-sen are less useful to plot, as the Senkou Span A is their average.

The common approach consists of checking where the price is compared to these levels. A green cloud and a Tenkan-sen above the Kijun-sen are seen as bullish signs and conversely. Lastly, these 4 lines give good levels of support and resistance; the longer they stay horizontal, the stronger the level.

Fibonacci

The Fibonacci sequence is a fascinating series of numbers that appears in many natural phenomena, including shells, flowers, solar systems and, yes, even the stock market.

It was named after the Italian mathematician Leonardo Fibonacci, who introduced the sequence to the western world in his book Liber Abaci in 1202.

The Fibonacci sequence starts with 0 and 1 and all subsequent numbers are equal to the sum of the two preceding ones.

| 0 | 1 | 1 | 2 | 3 | 5 | 8 | 13 | 21 | 34 | 55 | 89 | 144 | 233 | 377 | 610 | 987 | 1597 |

As you go higher in the sequence, you'll notice that the ratio of each number to the one before approaches a constant value, which is approximately 1.6180. This number is known as the golden ratio.

In this sequence, the number X_n represents 61.80% of X_{n+1} and 38.19% of X_{n+2}. These ratios will serve a to identify potential support and resistance levels for instance.

Fibonacci retracement

One of the most common ways to use those Fibonacci ratios is through Fibonacci retracement levels. Fibonacci retracement levels are horizontal lines that indicate areas of potential support or resistance. These levels will, therefore, give areas where prices may pull back or bounce off.

To draw Fibonacci retracement levels, we identify a swing low and a swing high in the price movement. We then consider the swing low as 0% and the high as 100%.

We can now draw horizontal lines at the Fibonacci retracement levels of 38.2%, 50% and 61.8%.

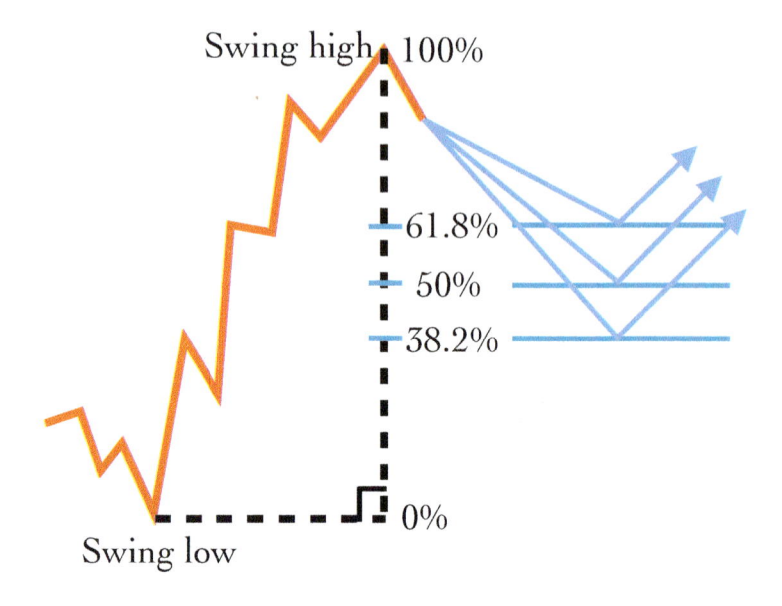

These three levels and mostly the 50%, indicate potential areas where the price may undergo a reversal and continue in its original direction. They can, therefore, be good entry points for your trades.

When it comes to long-term analysis, my personal recommendation is to use the level of 0.00 (currency) rather than the swing low and the all-time high:

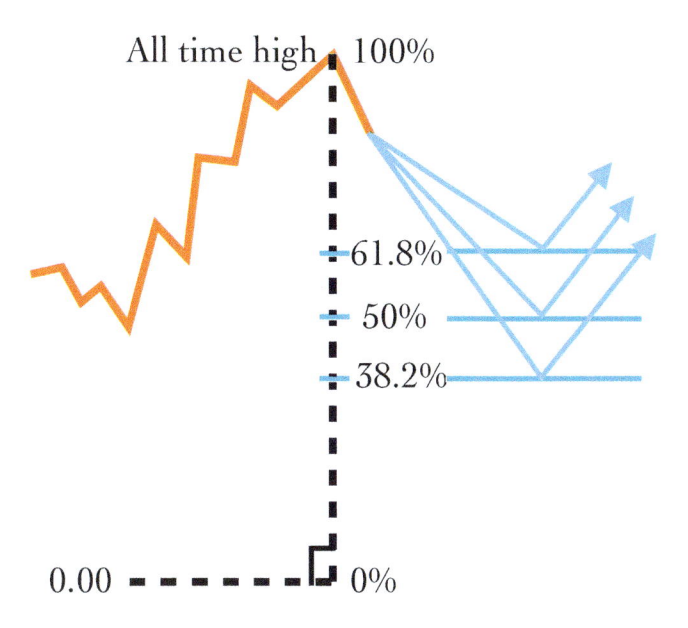

You might think that providing only three entry points is not satisfying; however, these levels are relatively close to each other, making it a valuable tool.

The method we just mentioned was useful to find entry points when the price is retracing to a level in which it has already been in the past. But how to find exit points?

The method we just mentioned is useful for finding entry points when the price is retracing to a level it has already been at in the past. However, it can also serve to find exit points. To find an exit point rather than entry points, we have to think of this tool in a reversed way - matching the three levels to levels given by the price. It is an uncommon approach.

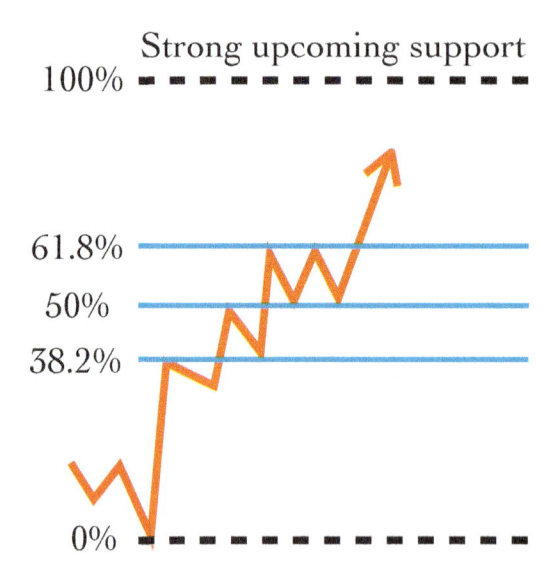

In conclusion, Fibonacci retracement levels can provide strong indications of potential support and resistance areas, which can assist in predicting price reversals. In addition to these levels, I find the 25% and 75% levels to be extremely powerful as well.

Fibonacci time zones

Fibonacci time zones are another way to use the Fibonacci sequence. Instead of tracing those levels horizontally, we trace them vertically along the time axis. The vertical lines indicate potential areas of price movement based on the Fibonacci ratios. We use these zones to identify potential periods of trend reversal.

To draw Fibonacci time zones, we typically identify key moments in the price movement, such as swing highs and/or swing lows. We then draw vertical lines according to the Fibonacci ratios of 1, 1.618, 2.618 and so on. These zones indicate potential periods of trend reversal and volatility.

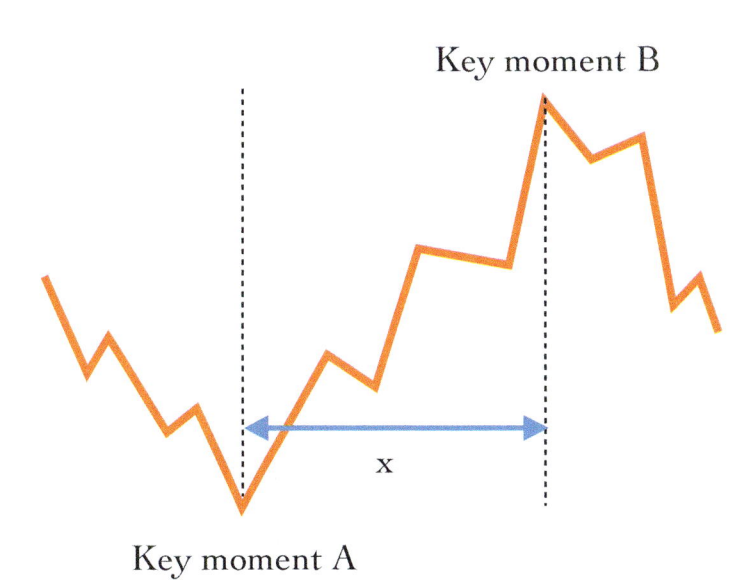

Key moment B

x

Key moment A

1.618x

x

Key moment C: there will be a peak or valley

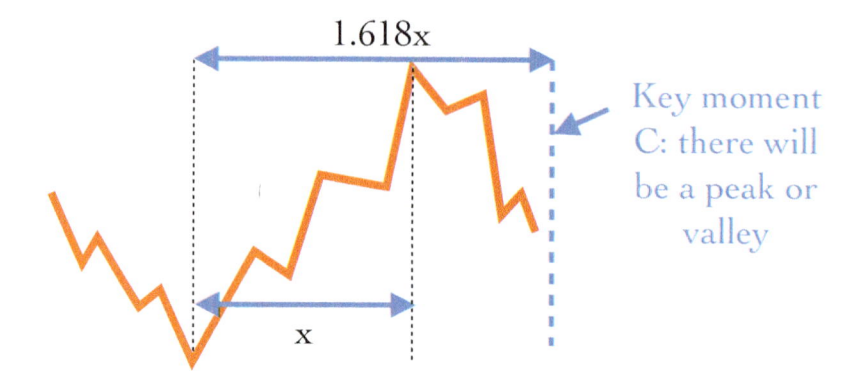

There are two scenarios: If the price is high by reaching our predicted key moment C, it suggests selling for a short-term strong drop. Conversely, if the price is low on C, it may indicate a potential buying opportunity.

← Sell

← Buy

Here's an example of a good trade with Fibonacci time zones.

Identify key moments

Get the distance

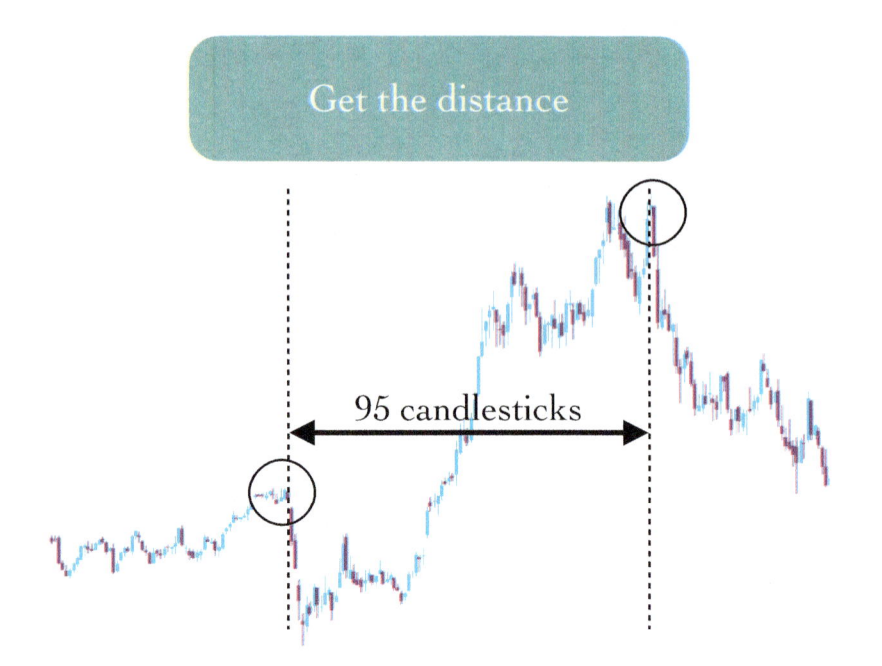

95 candlesticks

> Find the 1.618 level (multiply)

154 candlesticks

As you can see, the 1.618 key level hasn't been reached yet. Note the presence of a common gap pulling the price down. In this case, we have to wait to see if the price reaches the gap before the key level, meaning we would go long. If it doesn't reach it, we would go short.

Study

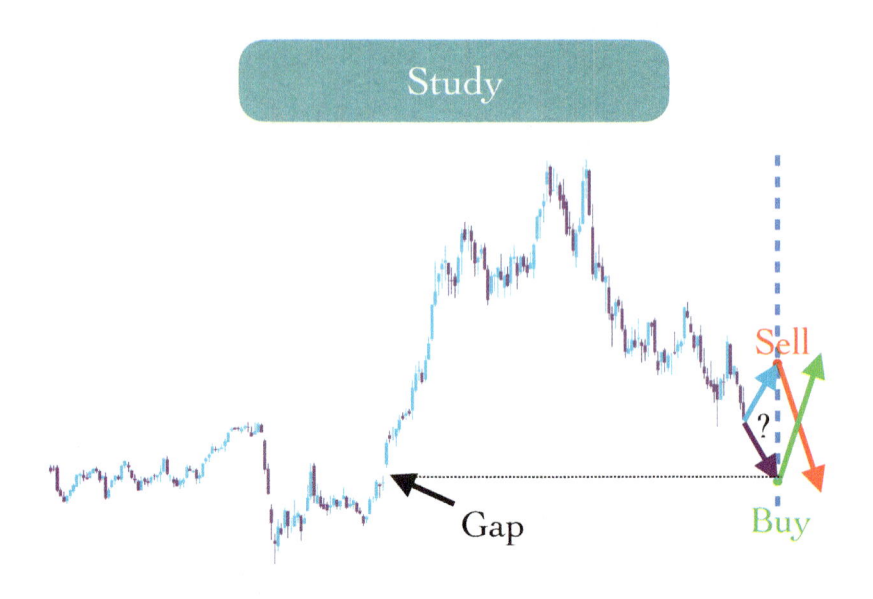

Gap

Sell
?
Buy

Result: we go short

In summary, the Fibonacci time zone levels provide a framework for understanding the rhythm and timing of market movements. At these levels, there will probably be either a peak or a valley. If, by reaching the level, you find the price high (likely to be a peak), then it would be a sell signal. If the price is low (likely to become a valley), it would be considered a buy signal. This technique is, of course, one among others; it doesn't work every time and should not be used alone.

In conclusion, Fibonacci ratios are a powerful tool in trading that can help you identify potential areas of support and resistance, determine entry and exit points for trades and identify potential periods of trend reversal and volatility. Fibonacci retracements and time zones are the most common ways for traders to apply Fibonacci ratios in their trading strategies. Also, keep in mind the importance of the 25% and 75% levels as well.

Fibonacci as periods

When it comes to the indicator's length, people commonly set the periods to tens or hundreds like 10, 20, 50, 100, or 200, for example, which works very well. We also mentioned previously that we can adapt our length in order to cover a week, a month, or a year, for instance.

However, it may be interesting to replace those numbers with Fibonacci sequence's numbers. Meaning using some of these values instead:

| 2 | 3 | 5 | 8 | 13 | 21 | 34 | 55 | 89 | 144 | 233 | 377 | 610 | 987 | 1597 |

For example, using a length of 13 instead of 14 for the RSI or 21 instead of 20. You can also opt for a moving average of 55 instead of 50. This approach can assist traders in aligning with Fibonacci numbers for those who believe in their uniqueness and potential.

My secret for periods

Here's my secret. My favorite sequence deviates from the traditional Fibonacci sequence. Instead of starting with 0 and 1, I initiate it with 0 and pi. Here's how it looks (rounded up):

| 0 | π | 3 | 6 | 9 | 16 | 25 | 41 | 66 | 107 | 173 | 280 | 452 | 732 | 1184 | 1916 | 3101 | 5017 |

Pi (3.14159...) is indeed a unique number and can be profitably applied in trading, along with other numbers like Euler's number, for example (2.71828...). This new sequence offers the advantage of providing fewer options to choose from compared to the traditional one, resulting in stronger signals. The ratio remains the same (1.6180), but the sequence is different.

This secret holds significant value for me. I believe it opens a gateway to the core magnificence of trading. By sharing it with you, I hope you'll be able to experience its value for yourself.

Multiplying

Finally, let's delve into an unconventional technique — multiplication. By multiplying the price swing-low or other metrics, we may uncover new and intriguing trading levels. In addition to Fibonacci ratios, key numbers for multiplication include 2 and pi.

Here's an example:

Bitcoin's peak in 2017 multiplied by pi gives the next peak of 2021

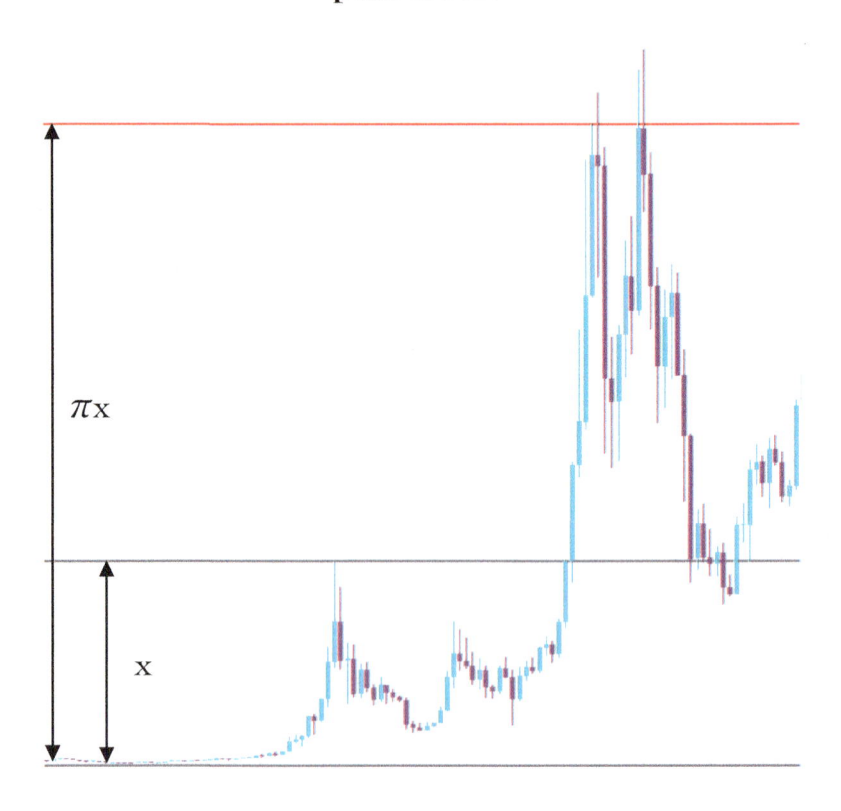

πx

x

It may seem somewhat unusual and that's because it is. Yet, surprisingly, this approach can yield results on occasion. Embracing diverse methods adds layers to our trading strategies and while this multiplication tactic may appear peculiar, it's a reminder that innovation often lies in the unexpected. There is no limit to chart analysis.

Elliott Wave Theory

Ralph Nelson Elliott founded the theory that market movements follow repetitive wave patterns.

Elliott categorized market movements into two broad wave structures: impulses and corrections. Impulse waves, comprising five sub-waves (labeled 1, 2, 3, 4, 5), represent the primary direction of the trend. Corrections, consisting of three sub-waves (A, B, C), temporarily counter the trend.

The theory emphasizes that waves create fractal patterns, forming both larger and smaller wave structures within a broader trend, offering traders insights into the market's cyclical nature.

From my point of view, it is better to simplify all this by realizing that trends are usually made of three impulses. The number 3 is crucial in chart analysis, as we will see in the next chapter as well.

The 3 impulses rule works best when spotting very fast moves. The approach to using them is simply by anticipating a third impulse when two have occurred or preparing for a reversal when spotting three impulses.

Study of impulses - FORD - Daily - 2018

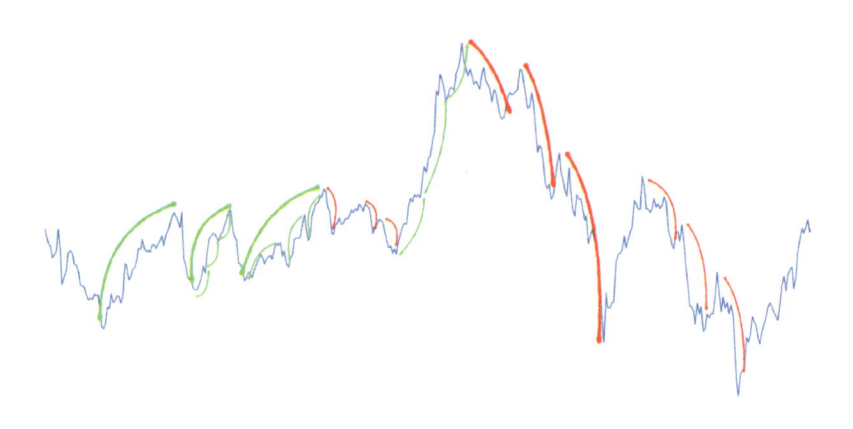

Study of impulses - RACE - Daily - 2021

Sometimes the magnitude of the impulses follows a sequence. For instance, if the second impulse is smaller than the first one, the third may be proportionally smaller as well and conversely.

Anchored VWAP

The anchored VWAP is a tool designed to calculate the volume-weighted average price since a given period. It allows starting the calculation from a specific point in the past. You should choose this anchored point based on significant events, such as earnings reports, major news, or crucial market turning points. It is a simple yet effective method for finding strong levels.

Anchored VWAP placed at the highest point

Chart patterns

Welcome to the final and perhaps the most interesting part of this book. Chart patterns offer a powerful means to comprehend the psychology influencing prices and to predict future trends.

The main challenge in learning trading often lies in the ambiguity associated with interpreting signals. We are taught that one signal signifies an upward movement, while another implies a downward trend, yet without accompanying probability. In this section, my aim is to provide concrete guidance, enabling you to establish probabilities for future price movements.

Let me reiterate, perfection isn't achievable in trading. However, these elements have profoundly impacted my trading journey, significantly enhancing my chart analysis skills. My hope is that they'll prove equally transformative for you.

The effect of timeframes on patterns

Before delving into these patterns, it's crucial to remind that the stock market is heavily manipulated and contains inherent noise. Consequently, the accuracy of the probabilities I shall provide diminishes as you opt for shorter timeframes. For instance, manipulating a 5-minute chart is unimaginably easier for institutional investors than manipulating a daily chart. From my experience, in a chart with a timeframe in minutes, false breakouts occur in about 50% of cases.

All the statistics I will provide below are derived from studies conducted in daily timeframes, realized by Thomas N. Bulkowski. Therefore, these patterns are likely to exhibit similar behavior in weekly or hourly timeframes.

Double top / bottom

The double top or double bottom is a widely recognized and powerful chart pattern resembling the shape of a "W" or inverted "W". These patterns emerge after a trend, marked by two peaks or valleys at nearly the same level. They signify that the asset has encountered a resistance level, signaling a weakening pressure from the trend.

This pattern purely concretizes the basics of trends we have seen previously. For instance, an uptrend is determined by higher highs and higher lows. When a double top occurs, we no longer have a higher high. If there is a good confirmation of a lower low, we take it as a sell signal. Therefore, it is even better when the second high is slightly lower than the first one.

Double top: 83% downtrend

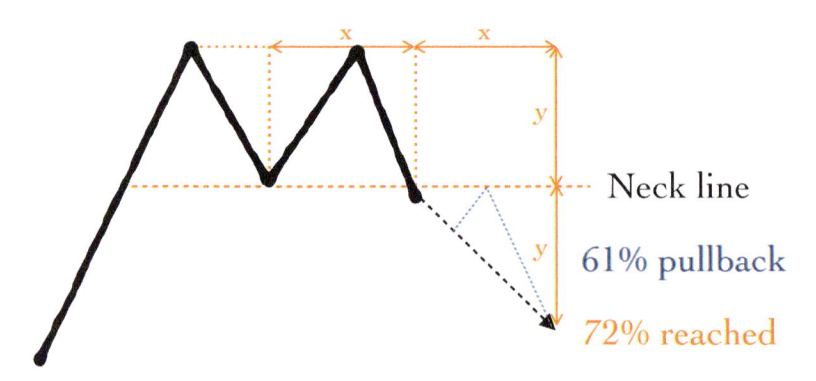

Neck line
61% pullback
72% reached

After a confirmed break below the neckline, prices tend to decline around 83% of the time. The frequent occurrence of pullbacks (61%) can make it wiser to consider the risk of missing the trade to sell when the pullback reaches the neckline. Waiting for the pullback also aids in obtaining better confirmation of the break. On average, the pullback reaches its peak at around 118% of the pattern's length (+18%). Approximately 72% of patterns with a confirmed break will reach the orange objective, which is a relatively good outcome. A bigger and secondary objective would be to correct the entire previous trend, although the likelihood of achieving it is lower.

Double bottom: 97% uptrend

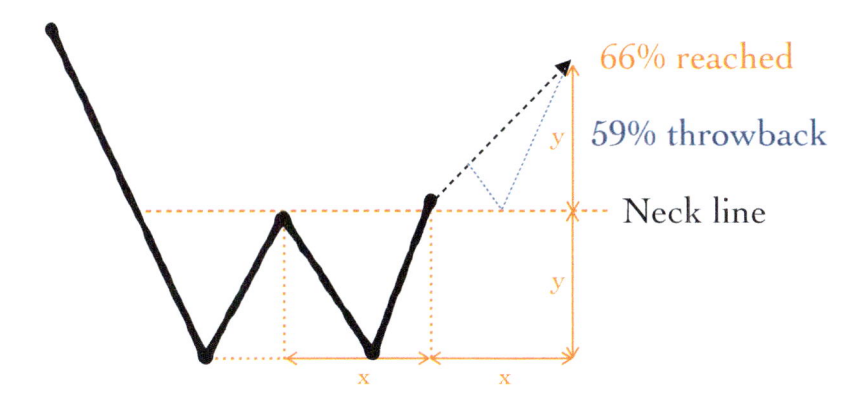

Following a confirmed break, prices typically decline around 97% of the time, which is very high. Considering the relatively high throwback rate, it is once more somewhat advisable to exercise patience and wait for this retracement. On average, the throwback occurs at approximately 115% of the pattern's length. Two out of three formations with a confirmed break should reach the objective.

Examples:

Double top without pullback - AAPL - 2h - May 2022

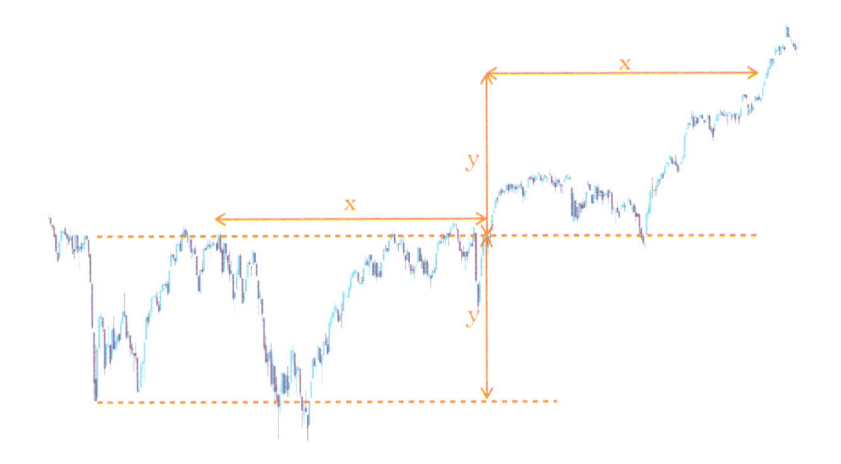

Big double bottom with two double bottoms on the lows - SPY - Daily - 2015

Lastly, keep in mind that these patterns need a previous trend and even after the break, there is a possibility that they form a third peak or valley. As we can see in the previous chart of the SPY, after the first big bottom, a double top appeared and broke the neckline, but it still went up to form a third peak, becoming a triple top.

Triple top / bottom

As we said in the Elliott Wave Theory chapter, the number 3 is very important in finance. Trends are quite often made of three impulses and a level rejected three times is a strong sign of reversal.

Three rejections: reversal signal

TSLA - August 2023

Going further:

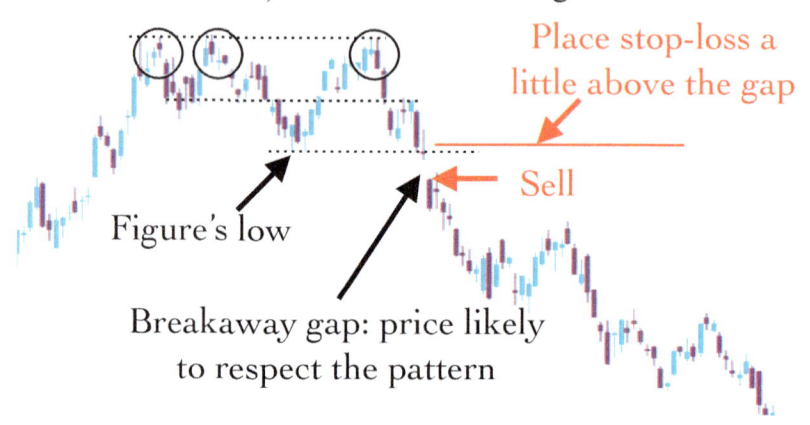

Three rejections: reversal signal

Place stop-loss a little above the gap

Sell

Figure's low

Breakaway gap: price likely to respect the pattern

This formation isn't a true triple top since the two lows are not at the same level. Nevertheless, it demonstrates that the number 3, in itself, can provide valuable insights into price behavior within your chart analysis.

As you understood, a triple top or triple bottom pattern is similar to the double top pattern, except it has three peaks/valleys instead of two. This pattern is not much more significant than the double top; however, its resistance and support levels are stronger.

Triple top: 85% downtrend

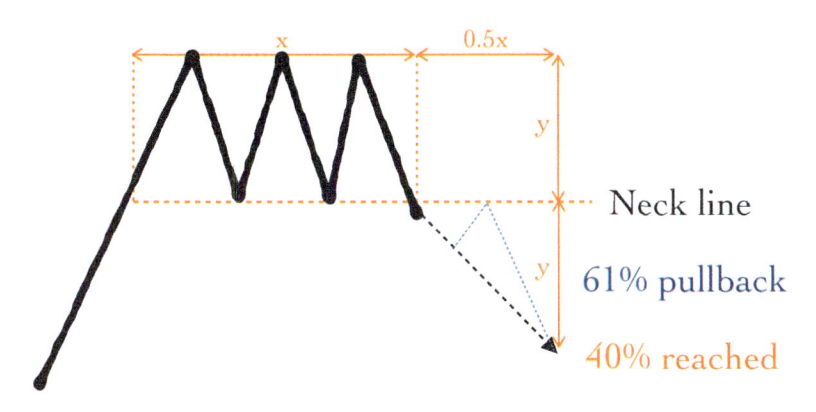

x
0.5x
y
Neck line
y
61% pullback
40% reached

After a confirmed break, prices typically decline around 85% of the time, which is quite a good ratio. Once more, the pullback rate is elevated. On average, the pullback reaches a peak approximately at 111% of the pattern's length. About 40% of the formations with a confirmed break should reach the objective, which is very low.

Triple bottom: 96% uptrend

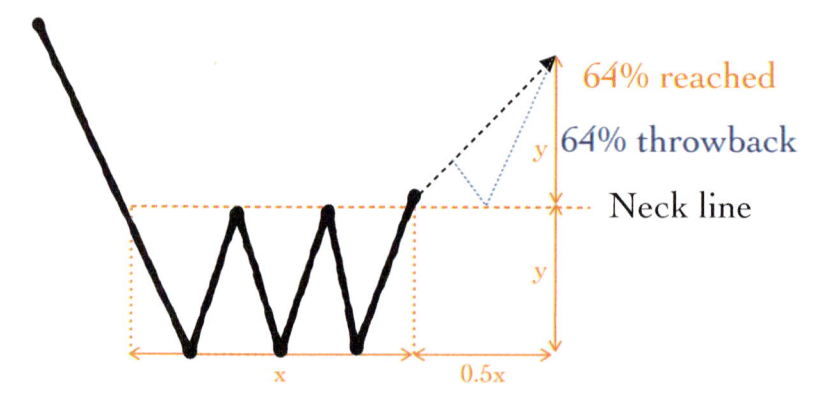

64% reached
64% throwback
Neck line

The triple bottom's strength lies in its high rate of uptrends (96%) and its throwback rate of 64% is significant. On average, the throwback reaches its peak at approximately 110% of the pattern's length. It reaches its objective about 2 out of 3 times.

Head and shoulders

The head and shoulders pattern is a variant of the triple top that still follows the principle of Dow's theory. Its strength lies in providing high predictability of the trend.

Head and Shoulder: 93% downtrend

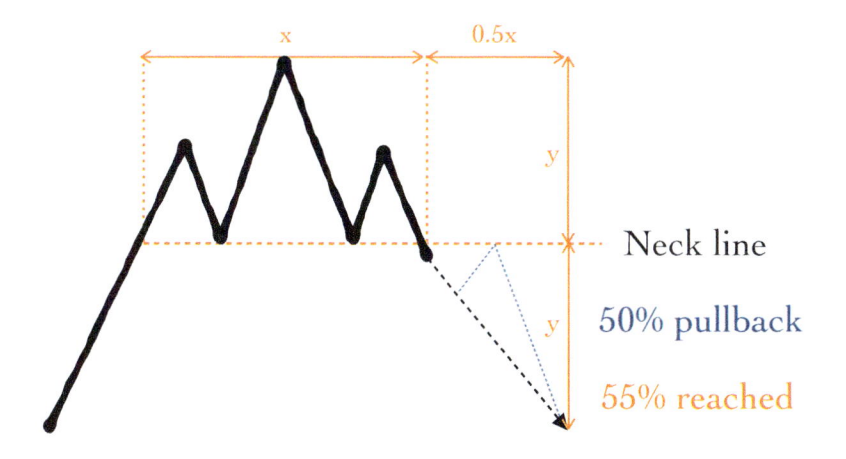

Neck line
50% pullback
55% reached

Half of these patterns will experience a pullback, typically reaching an average of 119% of the pattern's length. The objective should be reached in 55% of the cases.

Inverted Head and Shoulder: 98% uptrend

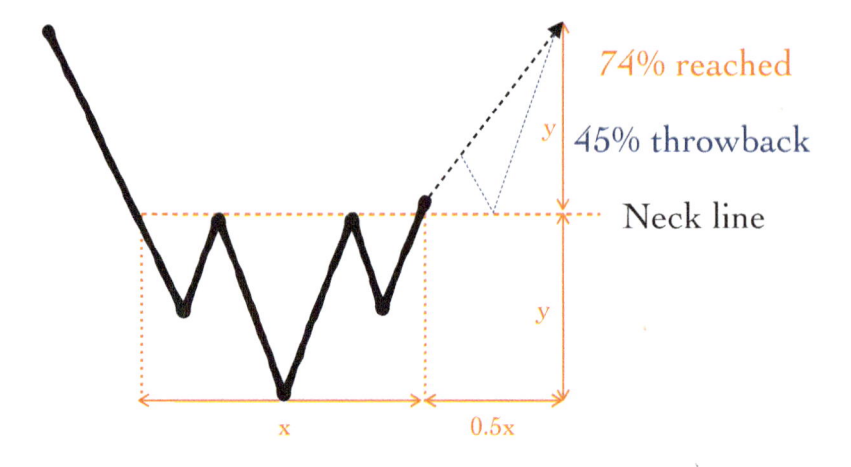

74% reached
45% throwback
Neck line

As you can see, the inverted head and shoulders pattern is more effective than the normal one. It reaches the objective 74% of the time and doesn't have as many throwbacks as compared to other patterns, typically occurring at an average of 116% of the figure's length.

Wedge

I favor patterns that provide a somewhat clear sign for the upcoming trend even before the breakout. Wedges are, in this regard, among my favorite patterns as they signal a potential exhaustion of the current trend. They occur when the price becomes confined between a resistance and a support, with both lines moving in the same direction (either upward or downward).

Base to apex breakout

A wedge's breakout occurs, on average, at 60% of the pattern's length. The specific terminology to describe the length of these triangular formations is the Base-Apex length, where the base marks the beginning of the triangle and the apex refers to the point where the two lines intersect.

Rising wedge: 82% downtrend

63% pullback

46% reached

Breakout at 60%

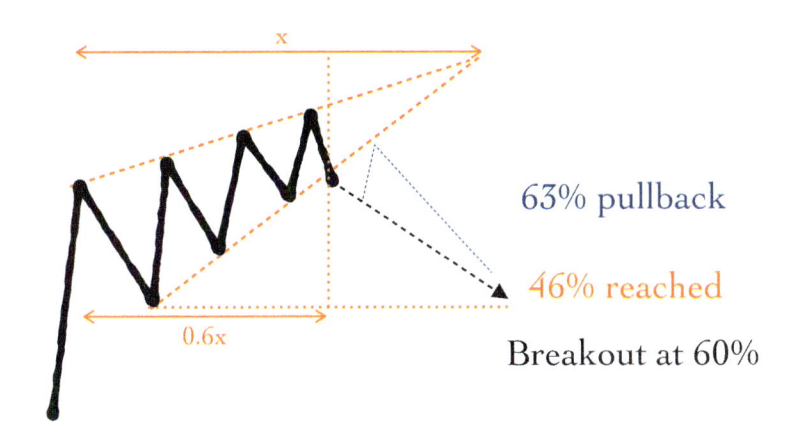

Rising wedges are a sign of an upcoming downtrend in 82% of the cases. They exhibit a high pullback rate of 63% at 124% of the pattern and often fall short of their target, achieving it only 46% of the time.

Falling wedge: 92% uptrend

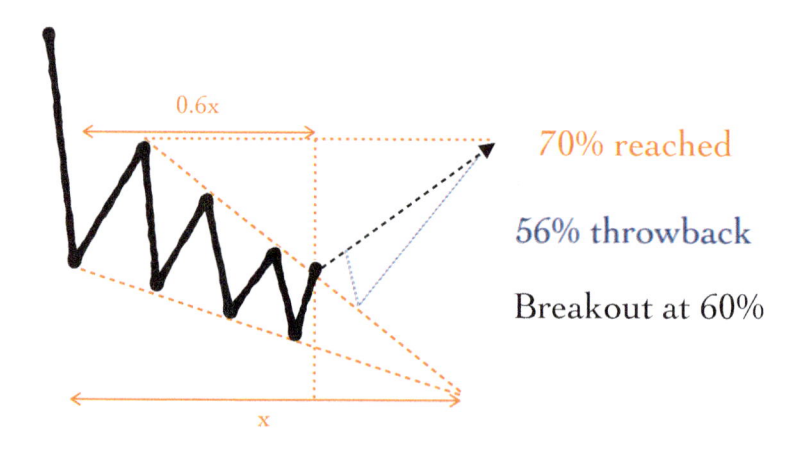

70% reached

56% throwback

Breakout at 60%

Falling wedges signal an uptrend in 92% of cases, which is a notably high percentage. With a 56% throwback on average at 123%, they achieve their goal 70% of the time.

As you can see, everything in trading is a double-edged sword: while we do get a very clear signal, the potential for gain is lower than many other patterns.

My personal approach with rising wedges involves placing my order in the middle of the resistance and the highest level of the pattern when we approach the 60%. As to the take-profit, I set it at the second-best level. Conversely, with falling wedges.

Example for rising wedge

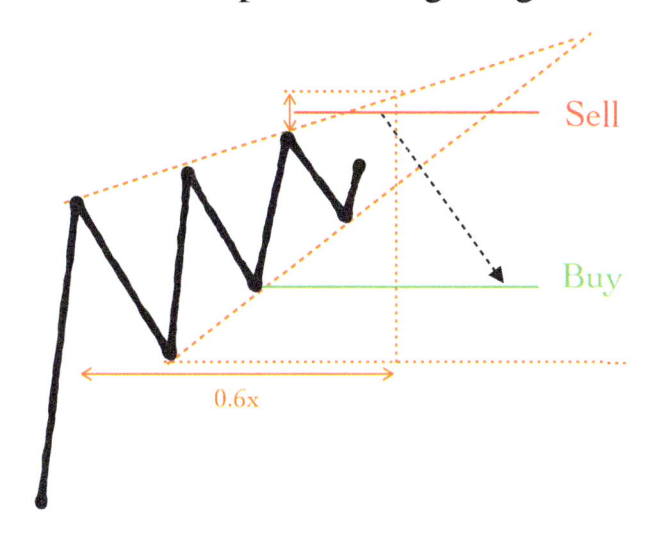

Lastly, you will sometimes find the three impulses rule within these patterns; in this case, the reversal sign is clearer.

Boardening wedge

The broadening wedge is also formed by two trend lines going in the same direction, but instead of being confined, the price's amplitude increases on every move.

Rising boardening wedge: 80% downtrend

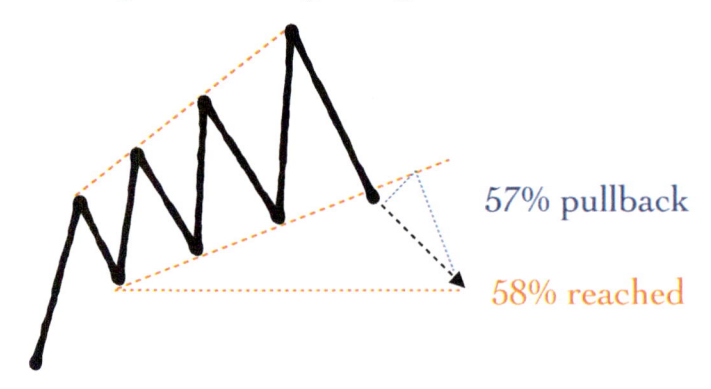

57% pullback
58% reached

With 80% of downtrends, the rising broadening wedge has a pullback rate of 57% on average at 110% of the pattern size, reaching its goal 58% of the time.

Falling boardening wedge: 79% uptrend

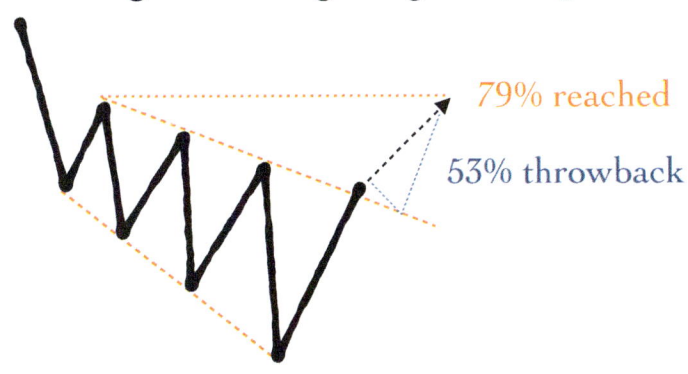

79% reached

53% throwback

The falling broadening wedge has a slightly lower throwback rate (53%), reached at 116% of the length. However, its success rate is much higher (79%).

Right-angled boardening wedge

The term "right-angled" refers to the fact that there is one horizontal line in the wedge.

R.A. Rising boardening wedge: 70% downtrend

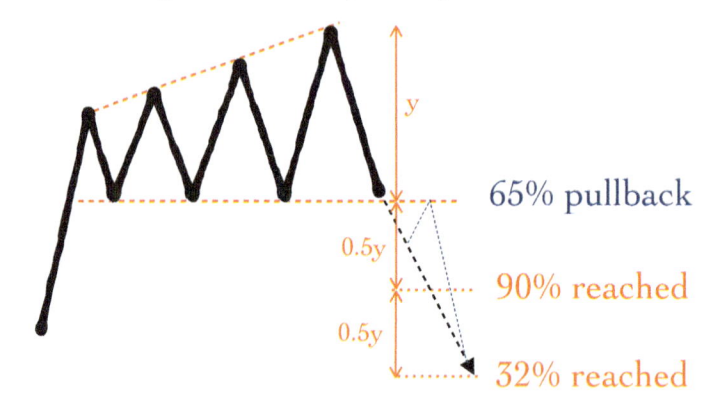

- 65% pullback
- 90% reached
- 32% reached

The right-angled rising broadening wedge is formed by an ascending trend line and a horizontal one. Showing a downtrend in 70% of the cases, its success rate is, however, very low for the standard target. It is therefore advisable to aim for half of it, as it is reached 90% of the time. Pullbacks are common on these patterns (65%), reached on average at 114% of the length.

R.A. Falling boardening wedge: 57% uptrend

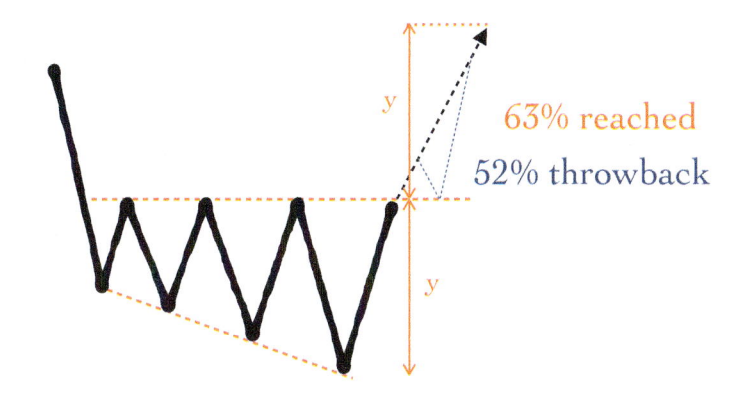

63% reached
52% throwback

When the pattern is falling, however, we can aim for a full target as it should be reached 63% of the time. On the other hand, its sign of an uptrend is weak, only 57%. A throwback occurs in 52% of the patterns, also at 114%.

Diamond

The diamond is also one of my favorite patterns. It is formed after a strong trend, with a horizontal period of expansion followed by compression. The shape created by this event resembles a square or lozenge. The shape has similarities with the head and shoulders pattern.

Top diamond: 80% downtrend

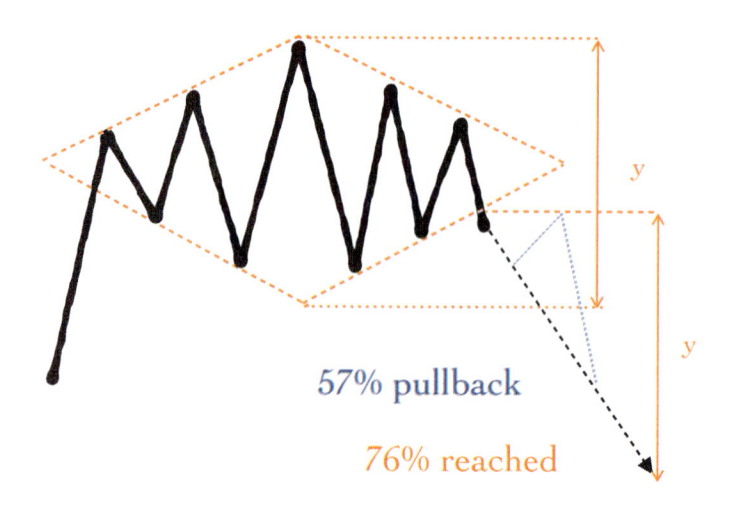

57% pullback

76% reached

The top diamond creates a downtrend in 80% of the cases, with a 57% pullback rate, reaching, on average, 120% of the pattern. Its objective is often achieved (76%).

Bottom diamond: 82% uptrend

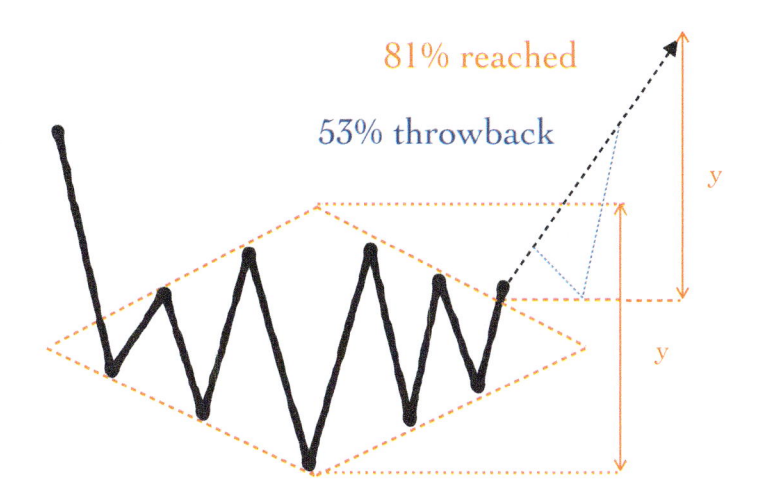

81% reached

53% throwback

As for the bottom diamond, its statistics are slightly better. The throwback takes more time to occur, on average at 131% of the pattern's length.

Triangle

The symmetrical triangle pattern itself does not give good indications as to the future trend. However, on average, the breakout takes place at 80% of the base-apex distance, which makes the future trend easier to spot when the price reaches this 80%. These patterns have many false breakouts, often recurring around 75% of the base apex. In clear, if you see a breakout at approximately 75%, you should be very cautious; if it occurs at 80% or after, false breakouts will be more rare.

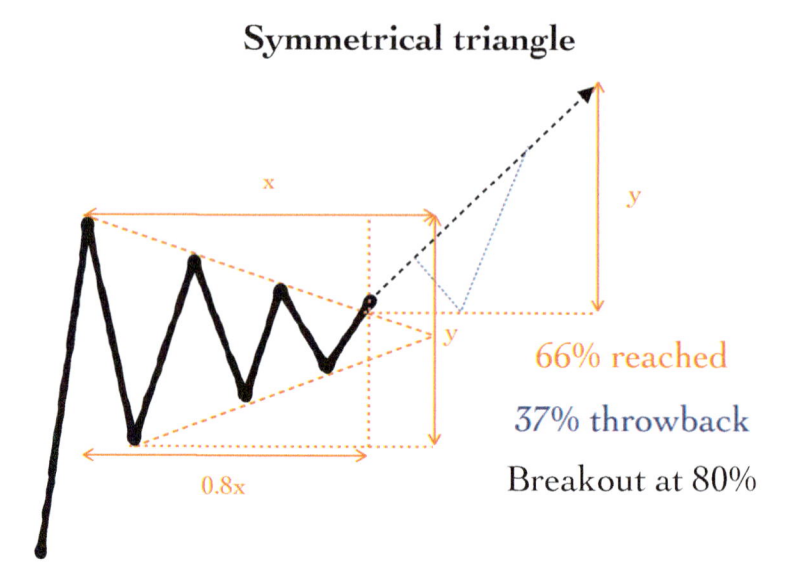

Symmetrical triangle

66% reached

37% throwback

Breakout at 80%

Two out of three symmetrical triangles will reach their objective. The pullback/throwback rate is only

37%, reached on average at 122% of the base-apex distance.

Ascending triangle: 62% uptrend

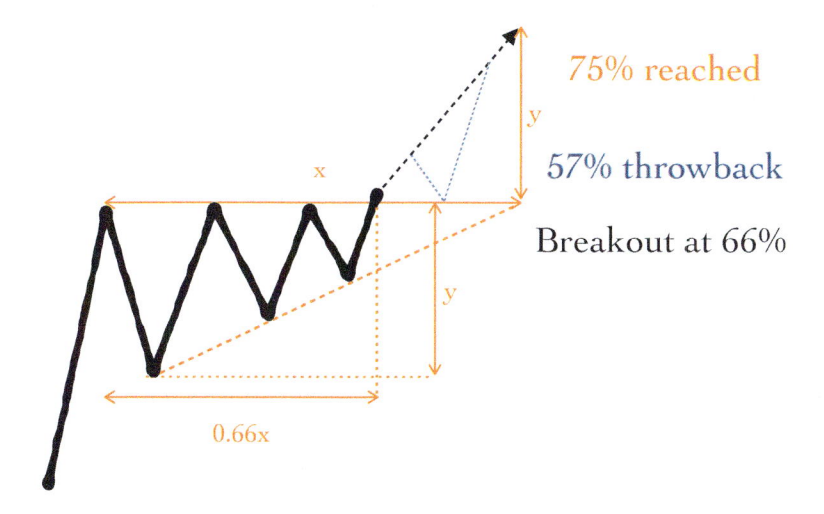

75% reached

57% throwback

Breakout at 66%

0.66x

The ascending triangle only results in an uptrend in 62% of the cases and three out of four reach their target. They have a throwback in 57% of the cases, reached at 120% of the pattern's length. The breakout should occur early, at around two-thirds of its length.

Descending triangle: 54% downtrend

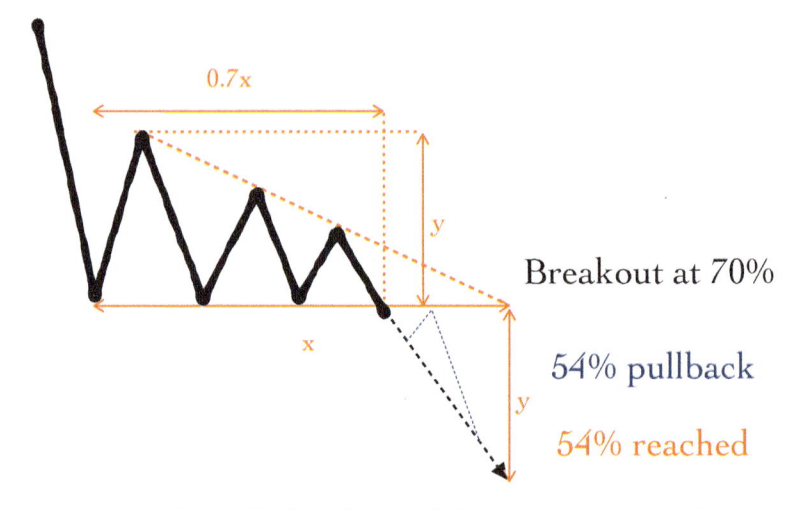

Breakout at 70%

54% pullback

54% reached

The fact that all the data of this pattern is 54% is not a mistake but a coincidence. The breakout in this case should occur at 70% of the pattern and if it makes a pullback, it should occur at 121% of the length.

Here's a summary of the information we just saw.

Dow's theory patterns

Pattern	Main trend	Main trend ratio	Pullback rate	Time for pullback	Goal reached rate
Double Top	Down	83%	61%	118%	72%
Double Bottom	Up	97%	59%	115%	66%
Triple Top	Down	85%	61%	111%	40%
Triple Bottom	Up	96%	64%	110%	64%
Head and Shoulders Tops	Down	93%	50%	119%	55%
Head and Shoulders Bottoms	Up	98%	45%	116%	74%

Exhaustion patterns

Pattern	Main trend	Main trend ratio	Pullback rate	Time for pullback	Goal reached rate
Rising wedge	Down	82%	63%	124%	46%
Falling wedge	Up	92%	56%	123%	70%
Rising boardening wedge	Down	80%	57%	110%	58%
Falling boardening wedge	Up	79%	53%	116%	79%
Right-angled rising boardening wedge	Down	70%	65%	114%	32%
Right-angled falling boardening wedge	Up	57%	52%	114%	63%

Diamond pattern

Pattern	Main trend	Main trend ratio	Pullback rate	Time for pullback	Goal reached rate
Diamond top	Down	80%	57%	120%	76%
Diamond bottom	Up	82%	53%	131%	81%

Triangle patterns

Pattern	Main trend	Main trend ratio	Pullback rate	Time for pullback	Goal reached rate	Break-out
Symmetrical triangle	None	-%	37%	122%	66%	80%
Ascending triangle	Up	62%	57%	120%	75%	66%
Descending triangle	Down	54%	54%	121%	54%	70%

Continuation chart patterns

There are many variations of the following patterns, they indicate a potential continuation in the main trend once the resistance is broken. These patterns are only effective when they are **small** compared to the preceding trend. Their objective can often be estimated by projecting the previous trend onto the break, similar to how we did for the runaway gap.

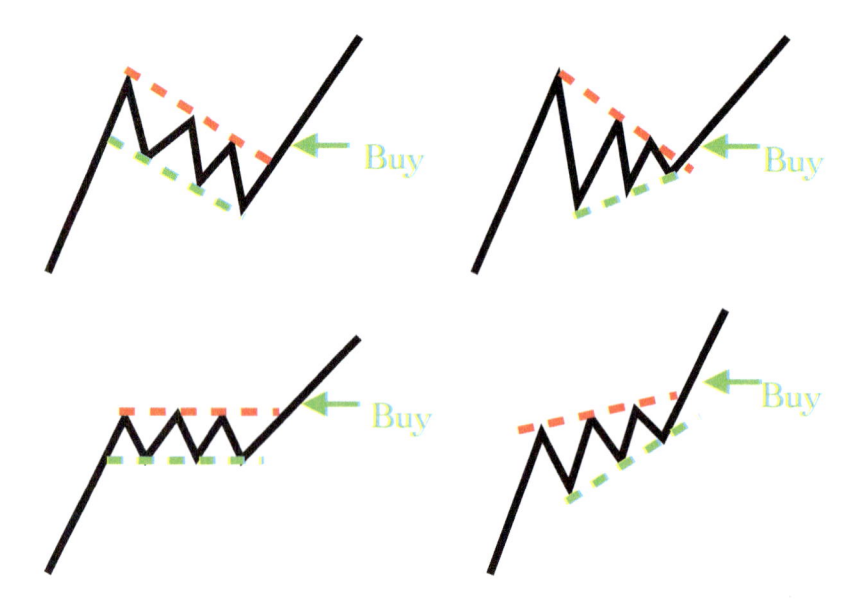

These patterns and their variations, serve as indicators of a temporary pause in price action before the trend resumes. They imply that the existing trend is likely to persist after the consolidation period concludes. However, it's crucial to exercise patience and wait for a clear breakout of the resistance before initiating any trades.

In this chapter of technical analysis, we delved into various chart-based techniques designed to enhance your market timing and comprehension of price movements. However, let's not forget the fundamental lesson from the introductory chapter: long-term investments serve as an excellent starting point for trading. The cardinal rule remains investing your money in safe yet profitable avenues, with the added emphasis on investing early.

"Time in the market is better than timing the market."

By staying invested for the long haul, you harness the power of compounding. While this chapter equipped you with valuable tools for chart exploration, it is crucial to pair these techniques with a long-term investment strategy to construct a successful trading portfolio. Even for active traders, allocating a non-reducible portion of your funds to long-term investments serves as a protective measure, reducing stress during short-term trading.

Lastly, keep in mind that technical analysis tools are not foolproof and they should be approached with caution. Their effectiveness is subjective, relying on the trader's interpretation and application. It's essential to practice and gain experience in them and to continuously refine our skills.

Final advices

If you've made it this far, it probably means that you appreciated the knowledge I shared in this book, and I couldn't be happier. I intentionally omitted some commonly used elements and indicators, such as the stochastic, the MACD, pivot points and some accountancy, focusing on what truly made a difference in my experience.

Let me share some key pieces of advice:

- See things as they are. Seek the truth.

- Listen to yourself.

- Be ready to lose.

- Consider what you would do if you were less scared.

- Rate your stress from 0 to 10. It should never be above 3.

- Don't be too greedy for money, be greedy to learn, greedy to make great choices that you won't regret and greedy to have an outstanding patience.

- Become an expert in a few or even just one asset. The finance world is extremely wide; learn all the basics of course, diversify as well, but aim to have an awesome local expertise (mine is Tesla, for instance).

- Keep calm and strong when you're in hell. Ensure your safety when you're in heaven.

And here are the biggest false beliefs on my opinion:

- The more you trade, the more money you make.

- The more complex, the more profitable.

- All price's moves are predictable.

- Trading requires a high level of intelligence.

To finish this book, I would like to give you my definition of what a trader is.

A jaguar is an animal that knows when to attack. They search calmly for their prey. Once they've found it, instead of chasing immediately, they wait. They wait for the perfect moment.

A good trader has a jaguar's acts.

A good investor has a turtle's mind.

The greatest successes will come by mixing these two.

You can do it.

Printed by Amazon Italia Logistica S.r.l.
Torrazza Piemonte (TO), Italy